JERRY FALWELL
and
THE JEWS

JERRY FALWELL
and
THE JEWS

MERRILL SIMON

With a Foreword by
Emanuel Rackman

JD | JONATHAN DAVID PUBLISHERS, INC.
MIDDLE VILLAGE, NEW YORK 11379

Address all inquiries to:
Jonathan David Publishers, Inc.
68-22 Eliot Avenue
Middle Village, New York 11379

1987   1986   1985   1984
10 9 8 7 6 5 4 3 2 1

Library of Congress Cataloging in Publication Data

Simon, Merrill.
  Jerry Falwell and the Jews.

  Includes index.
  1. Judaism—Relations—Christianity—1945-
—Addresses, essays, lectures.   2. Christianity and other
religions—Judaism—1945-   —Addresses, essays,
lectures.   3. Israel—Foreign opinion, American—
Addresses, essays, lectures.   4. Israel (Christian
theology)—Addresses, essays, lectures.   5. Falwell,
Jerry—Addresses, essays, lectures.   6. Moral Majority,
Inc.—Addresses, essays, lectures.   I. Title.
BM535.S52   1984   261.2'6   83-22266
ISBN 0-8246-0300-1

Printed in the United States of America

Acknowledgments

I wish to extend my profound gratitude to:

My wife, Amalia, who continues her loving support with understanding and patience.

Mr. Nelson Keener, Jerry Falwell's able assistant, for his help in seeing the project through to completion.

My secretary, Joan Gannett, for coordinating and preparing material for the book.

Dr. Jonathan Kolatch, for his invaluable advice.

Dedicated to
My son, Scott, and his wife, Devorah,
and my grandson, Yisroel Meir,

My daughter, Michal, and her husband, David,
and my granddaughter, Chanah Sarah.

Contents

Foreword

This book consists of questions and answers about matters vital to Jews. In my foreword I address myself to only three issues—the integrity of the interrogator, the reassuring answers of the respondent, and the sense of fairness of the reading public for whom the book is published.

The questions were asked by Merrill Simon—as loyal a Jew and Zionist as one could hope to find anywhere. He is totally committed to the survival of the Jewish people and the Jewish heritage. I hope that one day he will tell his life story. It will prove to be stranger than fiction.

The answers are from a man about whose role in American society many Jews have misgivings. Jews have been in the camp of the liberals so long that they cling to their erstwhile love even when it has forsaken them. However, the lovers of Israel today are to be found principally in the camp of Protestant Fundamentalists. And it is important that we know the views of one of their most prominent leaders. I find his views far from disturbing; indeed, I find them reassuring even if I differ with one point or another.

Fifty years ago we Jews did not believe Hitler when he told us precisely what evil he had in store for us. We erred badly and we paid a high price for our mistake. But that should not make us suspicious of those whose tidings are quite to the contrary—tidings for the ultimate success of our Zionist enterprise.

Merrill Simon is trying desperately to get Americans in general and Jews in particular to give Jerry Falwell a fair hearing. Is it fair to deny him his day before the court of public opinion?

Some of Falwell's views on sexual morality and the teaching of evolution in our schools do not conform to the attitudes of liberals. But true liberals should seek to protect the rights of majorities as well as minorities when freedom of expression is involved.

Indeed, it is in the interest of Jews to know precisely where we stand with our friends as with our enemies. And Mr. Simon is to be thanked for having obtained from Mr. Falwell the fullest expression to date of his views which from the perspective of Israel's security appear to be exceptionally benign.

Rabbi Emanuel Rackman

Bar-Ilan University
Ramat Gan, Israel

Introduction

The Six-Day War of June 1967 made American Jewry keenly aware of the centrality of Israel to their Jewishness. It began a six-year period of euphoria during which to be Jewish and to be pro-Israel was to be part of a mainstream—a rare period in Jewish history.

The surprise Egyptian-Syrian invasion on Yom Kippur Day 1973 brought all of this to an abrupt halt. With it, and the ensuing oil panic, began a systematic attempt by many of the world's opinion molders and governments to delegitimize the State of Israel. The prevailing climate enabled Israel's detractors to pursue policies toward the Arab-Israeli conflict which were neatly dubbed "evenhanded." Israel was now portrayed as the "bad guy" and the Arabs as the "good guys." Yom Kippur 1973 launched a painful decade for the State of Israel, world Jewry, and Israel's non-Jewish friends—a period in which Arab grievances have been dextrously legitimized with little attention paid to the historical context which spawned them.

In pursuit of perceived national interest, each succesive American president since Yom Kippur 1973 has
enlisted Americans of Jewish ancestry to help imple-
ment policies inimical to Israel's basic security under
the guise of "saving Israel from itself." The problems
of Arab oil and Arab money have forced each succesive
American administration to adopt policies based more
on the Middle East they would *prefer to see* than on *the
reality.*

During the past decade, those supporting Israel's
case before the bar of public opinion have dramatically
diminished in number. All of Black Africa, many of
whose countries enjoyed excellent relations with Israel in the early 1970s and were the recipients of Israeli
agricultural and technical aid, broke off formal contact
in an effort to line up on the right side of the Arabs. A
double standard of judgment has effectively been established: one for Israel and a second for the rest of the
nations of the world. The world noted with outrage
Israel's barely marginal role in the events at Sabra and
Shatila while paying no attention to similar Arab
slaughters of fellow Arabs at Damur and Homs and
Tel a-Zatar. The American Jewish leadership has
worked feverishly among friends and contacts made
during the heady 1967-73 years in an attempt to reverse the tide—but with limited success.

All of this has fed on and nourished a climate
increasingly hostile toward Israel. The National Council of Churches, for example, a body composed of the
liberal Christian Churches in America, has consistently embraced the PLO and the Arab position. Their
outspoken bias, and that of the Quakers and the
Brookings Institution and many others, has taken its
toll in bringing about an unprecedented erosion of

support for Israel within Jewish ranks. The need to appear conciliatory in the eyes of Gentile friends and acquaintances has caused them to seek a middle ground in an attempt to dissociate themselves from Israeli policies perceived by American opinion makers as fundamentally contrary to American or Western interests.

During this period, however, there has emerged one man who has become an outspoken supporter of Israel's policies and political positions, a person whose public support of the State of Israel has been tendered consistently, without apology, and without Jewish solicitation, no matter how controversial the issue. This man is Jerry Falwell.

Paradoxically, this support has not been well received. As Jerry Falwell's impact on American society has grown and as the American public has become increasingly aware of his extraordinary backing of the State of Israel and its policies, American Jewry and its leadership has become increasingly embarrassed, frightened, even confused by this strange bedfellow whose position on such moral issues as abortion puts him light-years away from the feelings of most Jews. Uncomfortable with "the enemy" as an ally, many within the American Jewish community have publicly theorized and privately speculated on the hidden meaning behind Falwell's unflinching love for the State of Israel. They have played down the sincerity of his "Zionism" by seeing it as a ploy to return all Jews to Israel so as to satisfy a New Testament precondition for the Second Coming of Christ. Some have gone so far as to attribute to Falwell a statement made by Reverend Bailey Smith before a National Affairs Briefing in Dallas, Texas, that God does not hear the prayers of Jews. Despite all of the criticism that Jerry Falwell has received from the Jewish establishment, he has never altered his pro-Israel stance.

Soon after the Yom Kippur war, it became very apparent that if Israel were to neutralize the political erosion that had taken place as a result of the oil and economic crises, a broader base of support than six million American Jews would be required. I felt very strongly that the basic good will of the Evangelical community—tens of millions strong—should be the first to be tapped. Their Fundamentalist view of the Old and New Testaments gave them at least a theoretical love of the State of Israel, which possibly could be transformed into a practical political support to offset the growing influence of the Arabs. At the very minimum, this would require a dialogue between elements of the American Jewish leadership and elements of the Evangelical Christian community. A Christian-Jewish dialogue of sorts had existed for many years, but only with liberal Protestants and Catholics, not with Evangelical Fundamentalists. In the spring of 1976, as national political editor of *Israel Today*, I wrote two articles explaining the need for such a dialogue.

It was within this context that I first met Reverend Jerry Falwell in the spring of 1980. Jerry Strober, Falwell's biographer and the author of a number of books on Evangelical ministers, agreed to arrange the meeting. We flew to Lynchburg, Virginia, to meet with Falwell. We had a pleasant lunch, a tour of the Liberty Baptist College campus of which Falwell is founder and chancellor, and a visit to the Thomas Road Baptist Church where Falwell preaches and from where his weekly television program—*The Old-Time Gospel Hour*—originates. The interview that followed appeared in *Israel Today* as well as in a number of other Anglo-Jewish weeklies. Several months later, I did a follow-up interview in Lynchburg. During subsequent meetings with Falwell and many conversations with his key aides, I became convinced that something had to be done to bring his affinity for Judaism and Israel to the attention of the non-Fundamentalist world. There was just too much misunderstanding and misperception within Jewish and Christian circles regarding his stance on issues vital to Jews.

It was in the fall of 1981 that I discussed with Falwell the possibility of writing a book which would clarify his position on Israel, Judaism, and the moral issues of concern to the American Jewish community—a book that would correct mistaken notions and perceptions of his views. I saw Jerry Falwell as a friend of the Jews, but I did not want to play the role of supporter, apologist, or interpreter of Jerry Falwell. The sole purpose of the book could only be to establish for the record where Falwell really stood on those issues that were vital to the American Jewish community.

We decided that the question-and-answer format would be best suited to achieve the basic objective of the book. Falwell agreed. He also agreed to one important stipulation: he would answer every relevant question put to him, no matter how controversial or embarrassing. He fulfilled his word.

I have found, throughout my contact with him, that he has been consistent in his expressed attitude towards Israel, Judaism, and the Jewish people. I feel secure in saying that this book presents the single voice with which he speaks to all constituencies. It cannot answer the question so often asked of me, "Does Jerry Falwell really mean what he says?" My answer to those of you who ask such a question is a quote from the Talmud which says that man can only judge another man by his deeds, but only God can interpret what is in man's heart.

Merrill Simon

February 1984

JERRY FALWELL
and
THE JEWS

Part One

FALWELL ON JUDAISM

1

Reverend Jerry Falwell is an Evangelical Fundamentalist Christian minister who accepts the word of
the Old and New Testaments literally and who believes, as a matter of faith, that personal salvation can
only come through the acceptance of Jesus Christ as
the savior of mankind. This one fact establishes an
insurmountable theological gulf between his thinking
and that of all Jews—orthodox, conservative, reform,
or atheist. To seek to bridge this gap is to attempt to
attain something which is not achievable.

What we can hope for is an understanding of how
Jews and Fundamentalist Christians differ, and precisely how these differences affect the way that the
two groups relate to each other. It is clear that there is
a lot of work to be done here. Jews have traditionally
held the feeling that Christians do not understand
them and, what is worse, do not *want* to understand
them. At the same time, many Jews have been guilty of
failing to make distinctions between Christian groups.
To them, a non-Jew is a non-Jew; all Christians are to

be lumped together. They tend to see no difference between Catholics, Evangelical Christians, and the liberal Protestant Church.

The problem in understanding Falwell's views on Jews and Judaism is twofold. The Jewish population in this country is concentrated in the large urban and suburban areas of the Northeast, the Midwest, and the Far West, while the Evangelical Protestant population is concentrated in the so-called Bible Belt: the rural Midwest, the Southeast, and the Southwest. Contact between the two groups has been and remains minimal, almost nonexistent. Jewish understanding of Falwell's positions has come through the popular press. And, because the liberal, large-city press has tended to feel estranged from Falwell— primarily because of his moral positions—it has tended to badly present and grossly misinterpret his views on Judaism and the Jewish people. The questions and answers in this chapter seek to clarify them.

I began my conversation with Jerry Falwell by asking him to recall his early encounters with Jews and Judaism.

Having been born and raised in a very small Virginia town, Lynchburg, with a very small Jewish population, I was actually a college graduate and the young pastor of a local church before coming into active contact with Judaism. Of course I knew what Judaism was. In my Biblical training in college we obviously studied all religions, including Judaism. But my relationship with rabbis and with Judaism in general began to evolve only as the scope and size of my ministry developed.

As a young Southerner, I had a very provincial attitude. In a primarily white and Protestant Southern town, most of us, including Jerry Falwell, were of a Waspish attitude. It was a number of years even after I was in the ministry of the Gospel before this provincialism began to disappear from my life and ministry. There are those people who say they were never prejudiced and have never held parochial ideas, but I doubt it. I personally give God, and my broad experience with a cosmopolitan society, credit for my emergence from that kind of philosophy and attitude. My study of the Bible from the moment of my conversion to Christianity gave me a theological commitment to the Jewish people and to the land of Israel.

I became a Christian four years after the State of Israel became a reality. There was never a time in my Christian life that I was not committed to Israel and the Jewish people theologically. But a number of years passed before I really began to look at Jews from the humanitarian perspective with which I look at my Christian brothers. I can't really point to the place and the time, but there came a day when I suddenly realized that this prejudice was no longer an issue with Jerry Falwell.

When all of that was flushed out of my system, my commitment to the Jewish people became more than theological. I began to internalize what the Jews had experienced for thousands of years. I began to realize the great need for Christian people, who claimed to believe in the Bible, to take what is often an unpopular stand and work to reverse the attitudes of a predominantly non-Jewish society against a very small segment of the world's population. There was a particular time in my life, perhaps about fifteen years ago, when this became an obsession with me. As a Zionist and as one who, in the Christian community, is probably the most outspoken supporter of Israel and the Jewish people the world over, I would say that I have become a radical on this issue. I think that radicalism is needed at this point in history to compensate for the injury that has been inflicted upon the Jewish family, often in the name of God, by religious zealots.

The South, in the past, has been known for its strident views on race and ethnicity. Many Southerners, and my family was no different, were raised to be what the media calls "rednecks." As a boy I never heard of Jews. If he was a Jew, he was always a "damn" Jew. Blacks were not known as Blacks in our area. They were known as "Niggers." This was common conversation. And it is very difficult for a boy to grow up in schools and communities with that attitude toward Jews, Catholics, and Blacks without digesting some of it into his own attitude and vocabulary. I believe there has been a natural evolution, throughout the South, away from this in recent years. I love the South. I love the people of the South. And I see a very healthy change sweeping over that part of our land. Unfortunately, in many of the major Northern cities I see a reversion to "redneckism" that has so plagued the South in years past.

What is your view on the "chosenness" of the Jewish people?

Some forty centuries ago God promised Abraham that he would be the founder of a special nation (Genesis 12:1-3). Over five hundred years later God directed Moses to lead that nation, then consisting of twelve tribes, out of Egypt into their special land Canaan (Exodus 1-14). In the days of Joshua, God led Israel into Canaan and established them in the land (Joshua 1-12). Although there were some rough times for Israel under the Judges, under many of the kings, and under foreign rulers, God has never abandoned His people. Moses predicted chastening for disobedience (Deuteronomy 28), which has occurred repeatedly, but the purpose for God's choosing of the Jew has never been revoked. Even during the awful spiritual decline experienced in Isaiah's day, God still said of Israel, "Ye are my witnesses, saith the Lord, and my servant whom I have chosen" (Isaiah 43:10). In fact, God repeated that declaration for double emphasis (v. 12). God chose the Jewish people to bear His name, to show forth His glory, and to be the channel through whom He would perform His will on this Earth.

For what purpose did God single out the Jews?

From all the earthly peoples, the sovereign God chose Israel to perform a twofold task for the remaining nations. First, they were to display the glory of God (Isaiah 60:1-3), and second, they were to convey a message of God. The Book of Jonah is a classic example of this second purpose. This choice, according to their own great lawgiver Moses, was not based upon any intrinsic goodness they possessed, but solely upon the grace and love of God (Deuteronomy 7:7-8).

So despite their "chosenness," you don't see the Jews in any way superior to other peoples?

No. In fact that is part of the apostle Paul's great argument in the Book of Romans. All men are equally lost and condemned before God—whether they be Jew or Gentile. Paul asked, "What then? are we better than they? No, in no wise: for we have before proved both Jews and Gentiles, that they are all under sin. As it is written (Psalm 14:1,3), there are none righteous, no, not one" (Romans 3:9-10). Paul went on to say, "For there is no difference between the Jew and the Greek: for the same Lord over all is rich unto all that call upon him. For whosoever shall call upon the name of the Lord shall be saved" (Romans 10:12-13).

A friend of mine wrote a book several years ago entitled *Christianity Is Jewish*. I believe that in the most profound sense. The Bible I believe, teach, and preach—both Old and New Testament—was written by forty men. At least thirty-nine of these men were Jews. Luke may have been Jewish. My Savior and Messiah, the Lord Jesus Christ, was and is Jewish. Whether tracing his lineage through Joseph or Mary, the genealogy traces directly back to David. Furthermore, I believe that the Old Testament and New Testament are inseparable. To me, as a traditional Christian, the Old Testament is the New Testament concealed, and the New Testament is the Old Testament revealed.

Neither Christianity nor Judaism is superior to the other. In my opinion, both are dependent upon the other and in need of each other. Judaism is yet looking for Messiah; Christianity believes Messiah has already come. But regardless, the Messiah being looked for by the Jews and being worshipped by Christians as having already come is the Messiah of the Old Testament—the book precious to both Christians and Jews. It is not inevitable that one religion be played off against the other.

Obviously, the Orthodox Rabbi feels that the Christian's Messiah has not come and therefore the Christian has no basic and vital faith. Obviously, the traditional Christian minister believes that Messiah has come and the Orthodox Rabbi did not recognize him, but is yet looking for Messiah to come. Neither view is anti-Semitic or anti-Christian. Both are matters of interpretation and based upon the views that each has derived from the Book of Books, the Bible.

And are the Jews still the chosen people?

Yes, very definitely. Although I believe that at the present time God's vehicle for world evangelism is the Church, Israel is yet to play a vital role among the nations. Israel is moving to the front and center of God's prophetic stage. I believe the times of the Gentiles (Luke 21:24) either ended with the Jewish taking of old Jerusalem in 1967, or will end in the not too distant future.

There are Christians who don't feel particularly kindly toward Jews, who will tell you that Jews give off an air of superiority, that Jews consider themselves better than non-Jews. Maybe there is something to this; maybe after being told since Bible times that they are better— that God chose them—Jews have developed a certain haughtiness; maybe Jews have brought their troubles on themselves?

Although such an attitude may be present with a few individuals from any people group, I do not feel this has been the case with the Jewish nation as a whole. Even if it were true, it would be nothing more than a surface cause at best. The real trouble has been brought about primarily because Satan desires to thwart God's purposes in the world. Since the Jew is such an integral part of that purpose, he is the object and recipient of Satan's counter-purposes.

How do you reconcile the Christian notion of the Church being the "assembly of the elect" with the chosenness of the Jews?

God was able to operate quite well before He chose Abraham and set apart the Jewish people for a place in His program. But having chosen the Jews, God's purposes for the rest of mankind were not cast aside. God often has plural purposes for various groups, and His goals for each group are always mutually compatible. Now, to my knowledge, nowhere is the Church ever referred to as the "assembly of the elect." Yet the

Apostle Peter used some of the terminology applied to Israel in Exodus 19:5-6 when addressing Christians in I Peter 2:9. He called Christians "a chosen generation, a royal priesthood, a holy nation, a peculiar people." This is similar to Exodus 19:5-6. Just as Israel was chosen, so is the Church. Their specific tasks are different, but both are chosen.

Could you define Christianity for us?

The word Christian appears but three times in the Bible. The references are Acts 11:26, Acts 26:28, and I Peter 4:16. It is interesting to note that in each case the word is associated with suffering and persecution, not suffering imposed upon Jews or pagans by Christians, but to the contrary, persecution imposed upon Christians because of their faith in Christ! Just what is a Christian? In John 3:3 and Acts 16:31 a Christian is defined as one who has asked Christ to save him from his sins and·has experienced the new birth. Jesus says the new birth is not optional. When one becomes a newborn Christian by accepting the death, burial, and resurrection of Christ as the atonement for his sins, he is "born again." The Holy Spirit takes up residence in his body. His sins are forgiven. He receives the promise of eternal life.

This newly converted Christian then becomes a part of the body of Christ—the spiritual family of God. He enters the communion of Christianity, by personal experience. One is not born a Christian. He does not inherit Christianity from his parents. He personally, by choice, receives Christ as his Lord and Savior.

Can you distinguish for us between a "Fundamentalist" Christian and an "Evangelical" Christian?

For a complete answer, you really should see my book *The Fundamentalist Phenomenon* (Doubleday, 1981) which gives the full background and history of both Fundamentalists and Evangelicals. In brief, however, both groups largely agree on matters of doctrine and belief. Disagreement is often in areas of methodology. Both, for example, believe that salvation is solely through heart belief in the efficacy of Christ's death, burial, and resurrection for man's sin.

However, in serving Christ, Fundamentalists have traditionally been separatists—that is, have separated themselves from worldliness and unbelief—while Evangelicals have not always been such. Further, Fundamentalists are generally more strident in addressing moral issues such as heterosexual and homosexual promiscuity, pornography, and abortion. Fundamentalists also take a stronger stand against doctrinal error and usually refuse to give support, financial or otherwise, to schools or ministries that allow a laxity in the area of theological and ecclesiastical purity. Fundamentalist Christians would compare somewhat with the position of Orthodox Jews—as far as strength of conviction and commitment to Biblical truth are concerned.

Could you explain for us the Christian Doctrine of the Rejection of the Jews and how Christians differ in its acceptance?

There is no such thing as a "Christian Doctrine of the Rejection of the Jews." When people talk of the rejection of the Jews, however, they mean God's original covenant with Abraham (Genesis 12) was unconditional and shall be fulfilled. But, at the same time, God's purposes for Israel may include some valleys to pass through before reaching the hilltops and plateaus. Because of its widespread present unbelief, Israel is largely set aside during the "Church age." There is still a believing "remnant" (Romans 11:5), and Paul definitely states that "God hath not cast away his people which he foreknew" (Romans 11:2).

Do you consider the destruction of the Second Temple (70 C.E.) as a sign of the rejection of the Jews?

There are several areas to consider here. Let me begin by saying I certainly do not believe a vengeful God inspired the Roman army to surround Jerusalem and brutally slaughter hundreds of thousands of Jews. It seems to me that even then the vicious serpent of anti-Semitism had raised its head. Satan would have liked to destroy the Jews in order to nullify God's promises to them. On the other hand, Christ Himself had predicted the destruction of Jerusalem, and He had done so with great sorrow and weeping (Matthew 23:37–39; 24:1–2; Luke 19:41–44). The destruction of the Second Temple did signify a change, however, in the basic approach to God. Men no longer came presenting their sacrifices to the priests, and the blood of animals was no longer sprinkled on the Ark of the Covenant on Yom Kippur. The New Testament Book of Hebrews draws some of these distinctions quite clearly, especially in chapters 7-9.

Although Israel has been set aside for a period, so to speak, her regathering is beginning and she will yet achieve a place of prominence among the nations of the earth. Jesus predicted a great future kingdom for Israel (Matthew 19:28; Luke 19:11-27; Acts 1:6-8). The time of that kingdom has not yet arrived (Matthew 25:31-32).

When you talk about a "great future kingdom," what do you mean? And when will it emerge?

When I speak of a great future kingdom for Israel, I am referring to what the prophets predicted in the Old Testament and has not yet been fulfilled. Just prior to Israel's great captivity in Assyria and in Babylon in the seventh and eighth centuries B.C.E., Isaiah, Micah, Amos, and others all foretold a coming great kingdom for Israel. Please read for yourself the following Scripture portions: Isaiah 2:1-5; 9:6-7; 11:1-16; Micah 4-5; Amos 7:11, 17; 9:9-15. After their predictions of both captivity and a final glory to follow, Solomon's Temple was destroyed (586 B.C.E.), and Israel has not had a kingdom since that time in the terms mentioned by the prophets. There will one day be a territory, a people, and a king. And the dominion and power of that king—the Messiah—will be total and universal. And all believing Jews will be a part of that great kingdom. Obviously, no human knows the time this kingdom will become a reality; only God knows this.

Wasn't the Holocaust an outcome of the idea of the rejection of the Jews?

I really don't feel this was the case. Hitler's attempts to annihilate the Jews stemmed from a personal not a theological basis. In his early days as a frustrated painter in Austria, his works were supposedly belittled by some Jewish art critics. If one adds to this his warped view of European history and geography, his insane lust for power, and a totally unstable mind, no theological reasons are needed to explain his actions. Furthermore, it must not be forgotten that hundreds of thousands of European Gentiles were murdered by the Nazis at the time of the Holocaust, as were multitudes of Christians of Jewish ancestry. He was not swayed by theological considerations, in my opinion. He was a madman.

What duty does the Christian have to counteract this "rejection complex"?

Christians need to show genuine love and concern for Jewish people just as God bids. God says He will bless those who bless the Jew, and He will curse those who curse the Jew (Genesis 12:1–3). The prophet Zechariah noted that whoever touched Israel touched "the apple of his eye" (Zechariah 2:8). As a Christian, I am commanded to make known to all persons, including the Jew, the good news of the way to heaven through the Messiah (Acts 1:8). Those are my marching orders. Peter told the Sanhedrin that "there is no other name under heaven given among men, whereby we must be saved" (Acts 4:12).

Paul expressed his love and concern for the Jewish brethren in these words, "Brethren, my heart's desire and prayer to God for Israel is that they might be saved. For I bear them record that they have a zeal of God, but not according to knowledge. For they being ignorant of God's righteousness, and going about to establish their own righteousness, have not submitted themselves unto the righteousness of God. For Christ is the end of the law for righteousness to every one that believeth" (Romans 10:1–4). Paul also made the point that "there is no difference between the Jew and the Greek: for the same lord over all is rich unto all that call upon him. For whoever shall call upon the name of the Lord shall be saved" (v. 12–13). Loving the Jew and sharing the Messiah with him is the most practical thing I can do for him on a personal basis.

In what way do you feel Christianity is an improvement over Judaism?

Improvement is the wrong word here. The New Testament teaches that Jesus Christ is actually the fulfillment of the Old Testament Messianic prophecies (John 1:45). Jesus clearly taught that He was the expected Jewish Messiah (John 4:25-26; Luke 24:25-27, 44-48). Christianity accepts the veracity of that claim. Thus, the entire background of Christianity is Jewish. We believe in a Jewish Messiah as prophesied in a Jewish book written by Jewish authors. We do not improve on Judaism, because it is the foundation for all Messianic fulfillment.

Let me then ask this another way. Christians see their religion as "Judaism plus," Judaism plus the New Testament tradition. That implies that Judaism without the plus is something less than Christianity, does it not?

Christianity and Judaism are not religions—they are revelations. Religion is man by his own efforts seeking in some way to reach God. Revelation is God seeking mankind and revealing to man his righteous requirements. Judaism is the revelation of God in the Old Testament. Christianity is His completed revelation in the New Testament. I would challenge every Jew to give the New Testament at least one good reading to see the relationship of both testaments. The New Testament takes only fifteen hours to read.

Is there, in your opinion, a better religion for Jews than Judaism?

Before I answer, let me ask a question of my own. Is a full-grown tree better than its original roots? The question is awkward, is it not, for of course the tree could not exist apart from its roots, nor could the roots fulfill the purpose of nature without the full-grown tree. What I am saying is that I view the New Testament as the fruits of the Old Testament, which are its roots. In other words, it is not a question of better religion, but of completed religion.

I would be less than honest if I did not state that I believe Jesus Christ is *"the* way, *the* truth and *the* life"* (John 14:6). Christ made this claim. Every committed Fundamentalist Christian would hold to this position.

However, it is my view that a healthy relationship between believing Jews and Christians cannot be achieved by demanding theological changes or revisions. We must accept each other as we are. We must candidly remain what we are. But, we must realize that, while we Christians, like Orthodox Jews, will continue teaching, preaching, and practicing our convictions, we can, at the same time, love one another and work together for many common goals such as the preservation of the State of Israel and the well-being of Jewish people everywhere.

The Jew, therefore, is practicing an "incomplete" religion.

Yes. Even according to his own standards—the Old Testament—the blood sacrifices are wholly missing. The Temple was destroyed by the Romans in 70 C.E. and the sacrificial offerings ceased. Yom Kippur is no longer practiced as commanded by God through Moses (Leviticus 16). The New Testament claims that

Christ, in fulfillment of the Old Testament types (prefigurations) and predictions (Isaiah 53) has *once and for all* offered up Himself as the sacrifice for all our sins. Whereas the Old Testament sacrifices were incomplete in that they had to be repeated yearly, Christ has "once suffered for sins, the just for the unjust, that he might bring us to God" (I Peter 3:18).

In light of your feelings about the Covenant and your commitment to the Jewish people, how would you react to the statement that was made at the National Affairs Briefing by Pastor Bailey Smith who said, "God Almighty does not hear the prayer of the Jew"?

How would I respond to it? I've done it at least five times a day since he made it! I think it was an unfortunate statement because it conveyed an arrogant and belligerent spirit when carried by the national media. If he had made that statement at First Baptist Church in Del City, Oklahoma, from a theological perspective, no significant rupture would have occurred between Christians and Jews. I happen to know Bailey Smith personally and I want to say this in his defense. He is a very gracious person. He is not anti-Semitic. He is not arrogant. He has long since corrected this schism. He has gone to the Jewish leadership and cleared the air. In a very positive way, God used this incident to build a bridge between him as the President of the Southern Baptist Convention representing 13 million Americans and the Jewish leadership. This bridge might not have been there if the crisis had not occurred.

So, if you want to know what I think about that statement, I am glad he made it. It forced a dialogue, something that had not occurred before, and resulted in good people coming together. As one man stated, "I didn't want to meet with those guys because I was afraid if I did I might like them and didn't want to." They got together and they did like each other.

Doesn't Christian theology state that the Law (Judaism) has been superseded by the new faith (Christianity)? Doesn't that in effect write off Judaism?

I am afraid your question contains several inaccuracies and also fails to take into consideration one of the key prophecies of Jeremiah. God Himself compared the Mosaic Old Covenant with a New Covenant which He promised to make with His people in a coming future day (Jeremiah 31:31–34). Naturally, every Orthodox Jew looks forward to and wants to be a part of that New Covenant. There is, however, a difference of opinion between Christians and Jews as to when the basis for this New Covenant was or shall be laid. Jesus claimed that His death was the basis for the New Covenant God will yet establish with Israel (Matthew 26:28).

Furthermore, let me say that contrary to what is perhaps popular opinion in the Orthodox Jewish community, Old Testament Law is highly esteemed in the New Testament. Note but a few of the references supporting this claim.

What shall we say then? Is the law sin? God

forbid. Nay, I had not known sin, but by the law: for I had not known lust, except the law had said, Thou shalt not covet. Wherefore the law is holy, and the commandment holy, and just, and good (Romans 7:7,12).

But we know that the law is good, if a man uses it lawfully (I Timothy 1:8).

In one of his epistles, Paul explains the relationship between Law and Grace:

Wherefore the law was our schoolmaster to bring us unto Christ, that we might be justified by faith. But after that faith is come, we are no longer under a schoolmaster (Galatians 3:24,25).

In other words, the situation concerning Old Testament Law is one of fulfillment in the New Testament and not one of abandonment. Christ Himself was careful to summarize this aspect during the Sermon on the Mount.

Think not that I am come to destroy the law, or the prophets: I am not come to destroy but to fulfill (Matthew 5:17).

Don't you feel that the very fact of Judaism as a living faith repudiates Paul's basic teaching that Judaism (the Law) could not thrive without the "new faith"?

No, I do not. As I have previously stated, the very existence of a thriving, worldwide, present-day Jewish community can be accounted for solely on the basis of the Old Testament promises of God to preserve Israel forever. But Paul pointed out several weaknesses of the Law also. The Law cannot save a man, but only condemn him (Romans 8:3-4). Only Christ can give life, not the Law. Otherwise, Christ died in vain (Galatians 2:21), and righteousness should have come through keeping the Law (Galatians 3:21). Unfortunately, no man who has ever attempted to could keep the Law (Galatians 3:10). That is why we Christians believe the vicarious death of Christ was absolutely essential to pay our sin debt in full and satisfy a holy God and Father. And further, this human depravity and weakness is recognized by the imparting of the Holy Spirit at Christian conversion to indwell the believer, thus enabling him to live the Christian life in the power of the Divine nature.

There are, within the Christian spectrum, those who believe that the Jews are responsible for the death of Christ. There are also those in the Christian community who believe that Christ was not murdered by the Jews, but died for the sins of all men. What is your position on the death of Christ?

I believe that Jesus Christ willingly laid down His life for the sins of all humanity. I feel that since we believe that He is God, He could have called legions of angels to deliver Him from the cross had He so wished. I believe He came to die. I think my sins were as much a cause of His death on the cross as the sins of any of the other 4½ billion people on this planet. I do not think anyone was responsible for the murder of Christ because I don't think Christ was murdered. I don't believe He was martyred. I believe that He willingly laid down His life and therefore that He made a Divine sacrifice for the human family.

Why, then, do you think that the myth of Jews as Christ-killers persists? Perhaps it serves some special purpose: the Jew as the universal scapegoat?

It has been my observation that those persons who refer to Jews as "Christ-killers" have a personal axe to grind—namely, anti-Semitism.

While it is true that Jews and Romans participated, humanly speaking, in the actual crucifying of Jesus Christ, all persons in every age must share in the blame for Christ's death. Christ willingly died, the just for the unjust. He laid down His life for all. In that spiritual sense, it is my conviction that, since we are all sinners, Jews and Gentiles, every human being in every age contributed to His crucifixion.

Do you acknowledge the part that Christianity has played in the persecution of the Jews down through the centuries?

With great sorrow and shame I surely do. Hiding under the guise of Christianity, dozens of pagan kings and their mercenary soldiers slaughtered both Jews and Arabs, especially in the Middle East centuries ago.

History however has clearly demonstrated that their goals of politics, power, and money bore no resemblance whatsoever to the many commands of true Christianity which absolutely forbid a Christian to treat human beings in an evil way.

But I think it should also be pointed out that had it not been for Bible-believing Christians, Hitler would have succeeded even more fully in his devilish programs. In addition, the *first* nation to recognize the State of Israel, and still its best friend, was America—a nominally "Christian" nation.

I think it is also vital to point out that throughout Church history, true Christians, like the Jews, have been slaughtered by political and religious pagans, all in the name of the cross. In fact, it may be said that the two most persecuted groups of people living today under communist regimes are Jews and Evangelical Christians.

And have New Testament teachings played no part in these slaughters?

While it is tragically true that untold multitudes of Jews have been slaughtered throughout history in the name of Christianity, the question must be asked: Can these murderous actions be justified by the New Testament? Let the words from its own pages answer this.

> Ye have heard that it was said by them of old time, Thou shalt not kill; and whosoever shall kill shall be in danger of the judgment: But I say unto you, That whosoever is angry with his brother with-

out a cause shall be in danger of the judgment:
and whosoever shall say to his brother, Raca,
shall be in danger of the council: but whosoever
shall say, Thou fool, shall be in danger of hell fire
(Matthew 5:21–22).

Recompense to no man evil for evil. Provide
things honest in the sight of all men. If it be
possible, as much as lieth in you, live peaceably
with all men.

Dearly beloved, avenge not yourselves, but
rather give place unto wrath: for it is written,
Vengeance is mine; I will repay, saith the Lord.

Therefore if thine enemy hunger, feed him; if he
thirst, give him drink: for in so doing thou shalt
heap coals of fire on his head.

Be not overcome of evil, but overcome evil with
good (Romans 12:17–21).

How did anti-Semitism develop and why has it woven itself into the very fabric of today's society, far outside the religious context?

I believe that anti-Semitism is not the product of
Christianity or any other religion for that matter. I
believe that anti-Semitism was produced by Satan
himself as an antithesis to the God of Heaven who
selected and ordained the Jewish people as His own
chosen family. The great controversy of the ages has
been God versus Satan. The Jewish people represent
the sovereignty, the grace, and the love of God.

Satan—and I do believe in a personal devil—hates God and all those who are selected and chosen of God. Therefore, it has been the personal campaign of the archenemy of God to hurt and, possibly, to destroy the Jewish people. When the effort was made in the days of Moses to kill Jewish children, it was Satan working through his emissaries upon this Earth. When Herod attempted the same thing, I believe it was Satan working through his representatives on this Earth. And whether we go back to the Pharaohs or the Caesars or to more modern times and mention Hitler and Andropov, I believe these men were and are spiritually motivated by the Prince of Darkness, Satan himself. I believe anti-Semitism is an antigod philosophy.

Do you feel responsible as a servant of the Church to oppose anti-Semitism?

I certainly do. In fact, I am commanded in the New Testament concerning this very thing.

Give none offence, neither to the Jews, nor to the Gentiles, nor to the church of God (1 Corinthians 10:32).

Do you think there is a way to stop anti-Jewish feelings in the name of Christianity?

One way to do this is to publicly identify all anti-Semitic groups which hide behind Christianity and expose them for what they really are: namely, hate groups, having absolutely no connection with true and genuine Christianity.

But the real battle can be won only as thousands of Christian ministers use their pulpits to decry anti-Semitism and to scripturally teach their people to love the Jews—and all people for that matter.

Christian educators, at every opportunity, should stress that Jews bear no responsibility for the death of Christ.

To what extent do you identify with the new type of theology that shows guilt-consciousness with regard to the Jews?

As a born-again Christian, I have great sorrow for the horrible sufferings the Jews have gone through, but not guilt. For, as I have already stated, *no* true follower of Christ was ever involved in that vicious slaughter record.

British professor of theology Rosemary Ruether claims that anti-Semitism is the "left hand" of traditional Christology. How do you react to this?

My immediate reaction is that she shows little knowledge concerning the difference between true Christianity and political Christendom. In any event, one theologian cannot speak for all Christians any more than a single rabbi could be said to speak for all Judaism.

Would you accept her suggestion that Christian theology needs a revision down to its very sources, including even the New Testament itself?

I surely would not! The basis for true and traditional Christianity is an inspired and inerrant Bible. Thus, what mortal has the right to change or modify the Word of God? The problem is not with the Biblical basis of Christianity. The problem is with those persons who, in the name of Christianity, misinterpret Scripture and twist it to justify their distorted ideas and philosophies—anti-Semitism being only one of those ulterior goals. It is important to internalize that *true* Christianity is based upon love, tolerance, and justice. Those bloody aberrations, whether the Crusades of the past or the present-day religious wars such as the Northern Ireland situation, are in no way representative of true Biblical Christianity. Christianity is nothing more than the scapegoat—being so used by wicked men.

What then is going to help the Jews?

I believe the only ultimate help for this wicked world comes from Almighty God, the God of the Bible. He alone is the answer to all peoples: Jews, Gentiles, black, white. God had very little trouble helping the Jews in Old Testament times, and I believe He can do just as well today. Jeremiah reminds us of God's promise, "Fear thou not, O Jacob my servant, saith the LORD: for I am with thee; for I will make a full end of all the nations whither I have driven thee; but I will not make a full end of thee, but correct thee in measure; yet will I not leave thee wholly unpunished" (Jeremiah 46:28).

But I also believe God uses human beings to carry out His programs on Earth. I personally feel a heavy responsibility to educate the American people on the importance of supporting the State of Israel and Jewish people everywhere. I am training thousands of pastors to do the same. At Liberty Baptist College, where I am Chancellor, and its schools, we are teaching 6,000 students the importance of this issue and how they can do their part in the future to stamp out anti-Semitism.

Don't you feel that in this secular age, anti-Semitism, though originating in Christianity, seems now to have gone beyond Christian control, leaving Christianity unable to deal with its results?

In my opinion, the major premise of this question completely lacks validity. Anti-Semitism did not originate in Christianity. Anti-Semitism began in *Egypt* (Exodus 1) because there God's promise of a "great nation" (Genesis 12:2) began to be fulfilled. The Old Testament Book of Esther records the efforts of wicked Haman to annihilate the entire Jewish nation. As previously stated, it is true that many persons have persecuted the Jews and done so allegedly in the name of Christianity. These were imposters. Every truly born-again Christian would deny any spiritual kinship with those so-called Christians who have hated and hurt the Jews.

I also do not believe that anti-Semitism is out of control in the United States. I personally believe the conservative Christian Church in America can effectively reverse this trend and can do so in this generation. I believe it is occurring right now. We have much to do—but we are winning as I see it. There are 70 million Evangelical/Fundamentalist Christians in America, according to Gallup. There are enough of us to make the difference.

How do you deal with anti-Semitism within your own ranks?

In our own ministry in Lynchburg, Virginia, we employ over two thousand associate pastors, teachers, and staff members. As far as I know, anti-Semitism has never once raised its ugly head among these dedicated workers. If it ever does, I would deal with it pointedly and promptly! We have 20,000 members in the Thomas Road Baptist Church in Lynchburg, Virginia, where I am the pastor. There are 7½ million families (approximately 25 million persons) on our mailing lists. These are persons who watch and listen to my television and radio programs and who write to me, support us financially and prayerfully, and stand with me theologically.

This represents over 10 percent of the population of this country. I daily—by radio, television, and the printed page—teach these millions of Americans the importance of taking a stand *against* anti-Semitism and *for* the Jewish people.

Do you consider a Christian who converts to Judaism as a loss to the Church?

I sense that you may be using the term "Christian" as equivalent to "Gentile." Although this is common among many Jews, it is not correct. Gentiles as such are not Christians. For a Gentile to accept Judaism is no loss to the Church because he was never a part of the Church. The very definition of a *Christian*, however, precludes the possibility of one converting to Judaism or any other religion. A Christian has become spiritually, vitally, and indissolubly united with the Lord Jesus Christ. Nothing can ever break that union (John 10:28–29; Romans 8:38–39).

What is your opinion of Christian mission among Jews?

The final words of Christ just prior to His ascension answer this question.

> But ye shall receive power, after that the Holy Ghost is come upon you: and ye shall be witnesses unto me both in Jerusalem, and in all Judea, and in Samaria, and unto the uttermost part of the earth (Acts 1:8).

It is my Biblical conviction that Christians are to

share their faith with all persons everywhere—not just with Jews. In our efforts to develop a strong alliance between Jews and conservative Christians, it is important to recognize and accept the fact that world evangelization is an irrevocable calling to the Church. There is nothing anti-Semitic about this evangelistic calling. To share Christ is a part of our faith.

And this you interpret as Divine sanction for Christians to go out and convert Jews?

Conversion is a spiritual transaction that takes place between God and man. It is not a task that can be either attempted or accomplished by men. Christians are to be obedient to Christ's commission to be witnesses and to proclaim the message that Christ died and rose again to save men from their sins. But it cannot be said that a Christian can "convert" anyone. Only as Jews and Gentiles hear and believe this message do they experience the spiritual rebirth commonly called conversion. It is actually God's impartation of a new spiritual life to a soul that has been characterized as spiritually "dead in sins and trespasses" (Ephesians 2:1-10).

So you see nothing wrong with Christians proselytizing among Jews?

I feel that on the airwaves, when Jews, Catholics, or Fundamentalists are preaching their particular doctrine, we are evangelizing. I think that is the uniqueness of the First Amendment right in this country. We all have that right. Two Mormon boys were visiting door to door in the street where I live recently, riding their bicycles, white shirt, black ties, and Mormon scriptures in hand. They were knocking on the doors of my people. I waited on the front porch for them to make the last house, where I live. They never got there. I assume someone said, "That's the preacher down there." But I would have liked to talk with them. Later I talked with a Mormon church leader and told him what I saw and expressed again the fact that I would die for the right of his missionaries to do that. However, I said one of our boys is coming to Utah shortly to start a Baptist church. And I would hope that you would fight for the right of my boy to do the same in Utah. I think the uniqueness of America is that Jewish rabbis can make approaches to Protestants and Catholics with their message without ever violating conscience or in any way causing hostilities to arise from our side of the camp. If a Jew listened to my message on the radio, television, or in person, and converted to Christianity, in my opinion there should be no outcry from Jewish leadership in this country because of that.

The airwaves are one thing. But how about direct approaches?

The early Church in the Book of Acts was comprised of converted Jews and Gentiles—both of whom proclaimed the Gospel to groups as well as individuals. It is my mandate as a Christian to do the same thing. My responsibility is to help proclaim the Gospel to every creature, Jew and Gentile, whether via the airways or via the direct approach.

How about the means used in trying to convert Jews. Do any means justify the ends?

An immoral means to a just end is, to my way of thinking, a contradiction in terms. In reality, of course, the mind of an individual cannot be coerced, even though some have used torture and other immoral means in order to obtain so-called "conversions." The means Christ authorized was the proclamation of the Gospel or good news about the salvation He freely offers to all who voluntarily choose to believe. It is my function to present that Gospel to individuals as well as to groups, and that is just what I do as God gives me the opportunities.

If a person truly embraces Christ as his Lord, he must do so voluntarily and intelligently—or no genuine conversion has occurred.

Are you and your Church aggressively seeking
to convert Jews to Christianity?

We have no such specialized ministry. We have no
Jewish mission operating in New York or anyplace
else. It is not because we are not interested in winning
everyone we can to Christ. But we don't specialize in
particular groups. We preach our Gospel universally
and we look on all people as people—not as Jews,
Catholics, unchurched, atheists. And as a result we are
successful in doing what we are doing. I feel groups
who believe that there are certain areas of the popu-
lace who must be zeroed-in on, are missing the commission of the Christian Gospel, which is to preach the
Gospel to everyone.

**What do you feel is the difference between a
Jew converting to Christianity and a Christian
converting to Judaism?**

I feel the difference is one between fulfillment and
abandonment. Let me explain. In my mind a Jew converting to Christianity does not abandon in the
slightest sense of the word his wonderful Old Testament heritage. In reality, a Christian Jew is simply a
son of Abraham who, having studied the evidence, has
concluded that Jesus Christ is indeed the Messiah so
often promised in the Old Testament. Thus, we see
the fulfillment aspect. But what of a professing Christian who converts to Judaism? This is an act of abandonment, for, after studying the evidence, he has
concluded that Jesus Christ was not the Son of God,

but was rather either a liar or a lunatic. He has demonstrated, in effect, that he never really *knew* Christ in the sense required to be considered a real Biblical Christian (Matthew 7:23). Therefore, in the strictest sense, this cannot be called abandonment—except in an intellectual way as opposed to spiritual.

Do you accept the Christian doctrine that the Church has come to replace the Jews and play their role in history?

Some theological and historical background is necessary here to properly answer this question. There exist today in Bible evangelical circles two main positions concerning Israel and the Church. One is known as Covenant Theology. This says, in effect, that the New Testament Church has, for all practical purposes, replaced Old Testament Israel as the vehicle of God. Another way of expressing this view is that Israel has become the Church. This view is arrived at by interpreting many key Old Testament passages in a non-literal fashion. Covenant Theology uses an allegorical method of interpretation to make some of God's great promises to Israel apply to the Church. Let me cite just a couple of such prophecies as an illustration of how this method is applied. In Ezekiel 37:15-28, God promises to regather dispersed Israel and reunite her in her own land under one king—namely, the Messiah. In Jeremiah 31:31-37 God also makes a new everlasting Covenant with Israel and Judah in which God promises to rule over them in their own land. Now if those passages are "spiritualized" to signify God's relation to the Church, then Israel as a people and a nation is left out. This is why those who hold such a position are not entirely supportive of the nation of Israel today. I personally do not hold this position.

The other view concerning Israel and the Church is known as Dispensational Theology. Those espousing this position are careful to maintain the biblical distinctions between Israel and the Church. Israel continued to exist after the Church was begun, and both have maintained separate identities to this very day. Even though their present roles are different, God has outlined a vast and glorious future for Israel. Israel will yet play a key role in the future events of this world.

The apostle Paul clearly explains all this in his great epistle to the Romans. Especially to be noted are chapters 9, 10 and 11.

- In Romans 9, he defends the sovereignty of God concerning Israel's selection in the past.

- In Romans 10, he defends the righteousness of God concerning Israel's rejection of Messiah at the present.

- In Romans 11, he defends the wisdom of God concerning Israel's restoration in the future.

Theologically, I identify myself with the position of Dispensational Theology. I do not accept the concept that the Church has come to replace the Jews and play their role in history. God has a separate, but mutually compatible, plan and purpose for both Israel and the Church.

Before leaving this discussion, let me quickly offer a final and vital observation. The rejection spoken of in Romans 10 in no way whatsoever implies there is some divine curse hanging over the head of each individual

Jew. In fact, to the contrary, the vast number of Christians in the early Church were of Jewish background, and all but one writer of the 27 New Testament books were Jewish. Luke was the only exception.

It would seem, therefore, that in your view the Jewish path is an "alternative" path rather than a "degenerate" path. Is that right?

I would agree that Judaism is not a "degenerate" path. But on the other hand, I would not characterize Judaism as an "alternative" path in the sense that it might lead one to the same destination as Christianity. Part of the stigma of Christianity is that it claims a uniqueness and an exclusiveness. Paul termed the message of salvation by means of the cross of Christ "a stumbling block" to the Jews, and "foolishness" to the Greeks (I Corinthians 1:23).

When Christ declared Himself *"the* way, *the* truth, and *the* life," He presented Himself as the exclusive means of salvation. I use the word "stigma" above because Christianity's claim of exclusivity offends many.

Why then has the Jew been so much the object of ridicule and persecution from earliest times down to this day?

The Jewish people are key to God's plans and purposes for this world. Satan is therefore perpetually committed to do harm to God's "chosen" people.

Do you subscribe to the view that anti-Semitism has been the glue which has held the Jewish people together? That it is so hard to be a Jew that without the constant effort on the part of non-Jews to remind Jews of their cursed fate, the bulk of Jews would have long ago assimilated?

The glue that has held the Jewish people together has been nothing but the sovereign purpose of God. God's promises to Israel in the Old Testament remain valid and will be kept with or without the presence of anti-Semitism. However, anti-Semitism has certainly drawn the Jewish people to each other as adversity always does in families and communities.

If the Church does not replace the Jews, what then is the purpose of its existence?

The purpose of the New Testament Church is similar to that of Old Testament Israel, namely, to display the glory of God (Ephesians 3:21) and to convey the message of God (Acts 1:8).

Given Church doctrine adhered to by some Christians regarding the Church replacing the Jews, can you see Jews and Christians living peacefully together?

Let me say again that as a dispensationalist I do not

believe that Christians are to replace the Jews. Beginning with Abraham, the first Jew, God dealt with man through Israel. Israel was front and center on the stage of God's program for man. The Jew was the repository of God's Divine revelation (the Bible) and an example of how God dealt with nations. Even though the Church has taken a prominent place in God's program since the first century C.E., God is not through with the Jew yet—nor will He ever be. I believe God is in the process of regathering the Jew to His promised land in fulfillment of Biblical promises (Genesis 12:1–3) and prophecies (Jeremiah 23:1–8). There is absolutely nothing in the Christian faith whether one is a covenant theologian or dispensationalist which would hinder in the least Jews and Christians from living peacefully together. On the contrary, there is much in the Christian faith and Judaism to draw us together.

Don't you feel that the theological view held by some Christians that the emergence of the Church spelled the end of the need for the Jewish people is bound to develop into social tension and intolerance, if not outright anti-Semitism?

I do not! I believe the fruit of anti-Semitism comes from the same corrupt root which produces all racial, ethnic, and religious hatred, and that is ignorance, intolerance, and a totally false concept of both God and man. Satan is the father of this hate. No *real* Christian should ever be guilty of anti-Semitism. The Apostle John wrote that Satan's wrath was and yet shall be directed against the Jews because of the coming of the Messiah through Israel (Revelation 12:5-6). According to Old Testament and New Testament prophecy, the worst time of anti-Semitism the world will ever know is yet in the future (Jeremiah 30:7; Daniel 12:1; Revelation 12:13-17). Satan will direct all his forces toward the destruction of the Jew. At this time, conservative Christians will prove to be the best friends the Jewish people have.

How do you explain the phenomenon of continued Jewish existence?

The present-day existence of millions of Jews in spite of unbelievable persecution from all directions during the past 35 centuries or more can only be accounted for through Divine intervention! As I have previously stated, God is not yet finished with the Jews. Their continued existence fits in perfectly with my understanding of their place in God's prophetic Scriptures. But as you can see, those who believe the Church has replaced Israel might find it more difficult to explain why Israel still exists today.

Israel's presence is perfectly compatible with my theology. Isaiah declared that "Israel shall be saved in the Lord with an everlasting salvation; ye shall not be ashamed nor confounded world without end" (Isaiah 45:17). I believe that prophecy will be fulfilled literally. In a similar fashion, Jeremiah wrote, "Fear thou not, O Jacob, my servant, saith the Lord; for I am with thee; for I will make a full end of all the nations to which I have driven thee; but I will not make a full end of thee, but correct thee in measure; yet will I not leave thee wholly unpunished" (Jeremiah 30:11). God will not allow Israel to be wiped off the face of the earth.

The point of continuing Jewish existence is therefore. . . ?

The point is simple: God keeps His word. Thousands of years ago, God promised Abraham that he would be the founder of a great nation (Genesis 12:1–3). God predicted that although the nation would eventually be scattered throughout the world (Deuteronomy 28:25, 64; Leviticus 26:33), it would nevertheless retain its identity (Leviticus 26:44; Jeremiah 32:40), and endure forever (Isaiah 66:22; Jeremiah 31:35–37). God's promises are completely trustworthy and certain, whether addressed to the Jew or to anyone else.

Is this sufficient reason to justify the existence of a people for more than 5,000 years?

How else can you explain it? God's purposes and promises are a sufficient enough answer for me.

How would you define the Jewish role in the world today?

Let me distinguish here between persons and politics—between the individual Jewish role and the role played by the State of Israel. I believe God desires the same basic things for individual Jews as He does for individual Gentiles: to raise their children to know their Creator. God is no respecter of persons. He loves all alike. He desires a personal relationship with every individual. The Bible is God's love letter to His people. And this Bible reveals the way of fellowship and communion with God.

Now concerning the State of Israel, I am convinced that the miracle of statehood in 1948 was providential in every sense of the word. God promised repeatedly in the Old Testament that He would regather the Jewish people unto the Land which He had promised to Abraham—namely, the land of Israel. He has kept His Word. The State of Israel is a constant testimony to the world that the God of Abraham, Isaac, and Jacob is alive and well. It is a reminder to all that God keeps His convenant with His people. The State of Israel, though small in geography and population, remains the focal point of history. All eyes are on Israel. And no earthly power, including the Soviet Union and one hundred million Arabs, can prevent the people of Israel from possessing their inheritance.

In what respect does this differ from the Jewish people's role in Bible times?

In the Old Testament their role was that of witnessing. Today it is that of waiting. But during this present period of waiting God invites individual Jews, as He does individual Gentiles, to come to Christ. Jesus said, "Come unto me, all ye that labor and are heavy laden, and I will give you rest" (Matthew 11:28).

You say that God invites individual Jews to come to Christ. Doesn't that imply that those who do not come to Christ—those who feel perfectly happy being Jewish—are missing something? Isn't this another way of saying: Judaism has its place, but accepting Christ—becoming Christian—is something better?

There are two questions here. In answer to the first, I would say, yes, I believe that the Jews—or anyone else without Christ—have a missing dimension in their lives. They are missing the joy and peace of having their sins freely forgiven and of knowing they are fully accepted by God. The answer to the second question is again yes. Becoming a real born-again Christian, based on an understanding of the Scriptures—both Old and New Testaments—is the best thing that can possibly happen to anyone.

What is the Second Coming and what does it mean to the Jews? Does it mean the end of Judaism?

To the traditional Christian, the Second Coming is the return of the Messiah who we believe came approximately 2,000 years ago, born of the Virgin Mary, in the Bethlehem manger. We believe that when the Messiah comes, He will catch away—rapture—the

Church, and those who have not accepted Messiah will be left behind for a seven-year period called in the Book of Daniel, the time of Jacob's trouble. We believe that during that seven years of tribulation on earth, during which time the Lord will prepare the earth for the establishment of the millennial reign of the Messiah, God will again appear to the Jewish people in a special way. From the Book of the Revelation, chapters 6-19, we perceive that 12,000 Jews from each of the 12 tribes of Israel—144,000 in totality—will again preach the Gospel of the Kingdom to all the earth.

We believe that God will manifest Himself to the Jewish nation at that time and that according to Romans, chapters 9, 10, and 11, the Book of the Revelation, as well as the Old Testament books of Zechariah and Ezekiel, the Jewish nation will believe on Messiah and, in the wording of Scripture: "A nation should be saved in a day." Rather than the end of Judaism, we Christians believe that it will be the most dramatic and glorious event ever for the Jew, as well as for the Christian.

What preparations must mortals make for the expected Second Coming of Christ?

No human preparations are demanded by God to bring about the Second Coming of Christ. Whatever requirements may be involved are of His own making. God has set the time for that glorious event, and He will bring it to pass. And no man knows the day or the hour of His Second Coming, Jesus declared in Matthew 24.

On what exactly does this Second Coming depend?

It depends upon no earthly event. In the fullness of God's time, Christ came to Bethlehem as the Lamb (Galatians 4:4). In the fullness of His time, Christ will come again to earth as the mighty Lion of Judah and King of Kings (Revelation 19:11–16).

I believe the Second Coming of Christ is composed of two aspects. At any time, in a completely imminent fashion, Christ will return to resurrect the dead bodies of all Christians who have died since His first coming. In addition, concurrent with the resurrection of those dead saints, all living persons who have trusted Christ for their personal salvation will be taken up with Him to return to Heaven. After that initial event, a period of great Tribulation (Jeremiah 30:7) will overtake the remainder of Earth's population for a period of seven years. Then Christ shall again return with His saints to judge the people of the Earth and to establish His Kingdom (Zechariah 14).

Is it part of your theology to believe that the Jews in Israel will eventually accept Jesus and thus usher in the Second Coming? Is the Second Coming in your opinion theologically predicated upon Jews converting to Christianity?

I don't believe anything has to happen before what we call the Second Coming or the Second Advent of Christ occurs. Neither the salvation of the Jewish

passages which speak of the Jews with condescension. In fact, to the contrary, Paul elevates them. Note his language:

> What advantage then hath the Jew? Or what profit is there of circumcision? Much every way: chiefly, because that unto them were committed the oracles of God (Romans 3:1,2).

How would you explain to your followers texts which mention the Jews as "killers of Christ and the prophets" (I Thessalonians 2:15)?

Initially, let me point out that this verse should correctly read that the Jews "both killed the Lord Jesus, and their own prophets," meaning the Old Testament prophets. Paul mentioned this in a context of warning about persecution—which he and other Christians were suffering at the hands of unbelieving Gentiles as well as Jews. And while it is true that the same apostle who had previously elevated Israel also points out their crime of killing their Messiah, several factors must be kept in mind.

First, no statement from Paul could be considered anti-Semitic, for he himself was a Hebrew of the Hebrews (see Philippians 3:4-6).

Second, his personal view of his own people was a compassionate one. In fact, he once testified of his willingness to become accursed by God, if this act could lead to the spiritual benefit of Israel (Romans 9:1-3).

Third, the New Testament makes very clear the

part wicked Gentiles played in the death of Christ. It was, after all, the Gentile governor Pilate who sentenced Him to die, together with Herod Agrippa's plotting, and the Romans who actually nailed Him to the cross. Acts 4:27 makes this very clear.

Fourth, the death of Christ in the New Testament is never pictured in terms of simply a religious teacher being brutally murdered by a mob, be they Jews or Gentiles, but rather the free act of a sinless redeemer who willingly laid down His life for all people. This is clearly brought out by the following verses:

> For God so loved the world, that he gave his only begotten Son, that whosoever believeth in him should not perish, but have everlasting life (John 3:16).

> No man taketh it from me, but I lay it down myself. I have power to lay it down, and I have power to take it away. This commandment have I received of my Father (John 10:18).

Finally, and perhaps most importantly, the Scriptures make it abundantly clear that Christ died because of the sins of us all. No one is exempted from the guilt that caused Him to die for all men (Isaiah 53:4-6; I Corinthians 15:3). Each of us had his or her own part in His death.

How would you explain the verse in St. John 8:44 that describes the seed of Abraham, that is, the Jews, as having the devil for a father and as not being capable of discerning truth?

This verse must be seen in its full context to be

understood. Christ directed these words to a group of Pharisees, and not to Jews in general. All through His public life He had been hounded by them. In fact, in this very chapter (John 8) they had referred to Him as a devil (v. 52), and took up stones to kill Him (v. 59). The truth is, He was, in general, well received by the common Jewish person. For nearly four years He had healed their sick, blessed their children, and comforted their hearts.

What exactly is the thrust of these verses?

The thrust is simple—a relatively small group of Jewish leaders made a tragic mistake when they condemned their Messiah and delivered Him over to the Roman authorities for crucifixion.

Was this just a blunder, or was it a forever unpardonable sin; the type of sin which has tagged Jews everywhere as "Christ killers," and bred anti-Semitism into the fabric of human civilization?

The only sin that is unpardonable is to die without Christ as one's Savior. All other sins can and have been forgiven. The condemnation and crucifixion of Christ by Jewish and Roman leaders was a tragic error of judgment. But many of those same individuals who called for Christ's death later asked for and received forgiveness (Acts 6:7). In the same manner, over the centuries many Gentiles have made a tragic blunder in judgment by practicing anti-Semitism or any other form of prejudice. I believe that men may be forgiven and delivered from the latter as well.

Do you consider the New Testament as God-inspired?

Absolutely. I subscribe to the verbal-plenary view of inspiration concerning both the Old and the New Testament. This says, in effect, that every single Biblical word in its original writing was directly given to the human authors by the Holy Spirit of God. Both the process and the product were without any omissions, additions, or errors of any kind.

If you do consider the New Testament to be God-inspired, how do you explain the presence within its pages of the type of reference to the Jews just cited?

Because it is the word of God, the Bible is an unedited, unabridged, and accurate account of those human and Divine events it described. The sins of both Jews and Gentiles are recorded, along with the extended grace of God to each group.

Do you see a threat to Christianity and to the fulfillment of prophecy from the rise of Islamic Fundamentalism in the shape it is taking today?

Islamic Fundamentalism is one of the most dangerous movements on the face of the earth. Any Christian missionary in any Moslem land can tell you that this is true. It is very difficult to exist physically as a Christian missionary in a strongly Fundamentalist Moslem country. I feel that the spread of Fundamentalist Islamic religion must be looked on as a very dangerous phenomenon in the 1980s.

Do you take a man like Qaddafi seriously when he calls for the conversion of all Christian Arabs to Islam?

Yes, I take him very seriously. The Moslem religion is making terrific inroads among black Americans and, while every Christian minister should have a deep love for every human being, which would include Shiite Moslems as individuals, we cannot ignore the fact that if such a Shiite religion were in the 51 percent majority in America, we could expect the same treatment as is being given to non-Moslems in Iran today.

Do you believe that there is a basis for a Jewish-Christian dialogue on theological matters? If so, what nature should this dialogue take and what stands in its path?

I have personally both welcomed and sought out every possible opportunity afforded me to address various elements within the Jewish community, if for no other reason than to reassure them of my own support of Israel and my concern about anti-Semitism in this country.

Several obstacles hinder an open dialogue between Conservative Evangelicals, Protestant Christians, and the Jewish community. The Jews very understandably look at the Evangelistic commitments of the Conservative Church as obnoxious. At the same time, Evangelicals and Fundamentalists feel that we have a commission from the Lord Jesus Christ to share the Gospel with every person in our generation. Another obstacle would be that many Christians feel that it would be a theological compromise to sit down with a people who deny the existence of our Savior and Messiah. In my opinion, these obstacles can be overcome without theological compromise if both parties are willing to accept the other as they are and not as we wish they were.

Christians can never change their commitment toward Evangelization. Judaism, in its truest sense, can never honestly accept a Messiah who they believe did not come. Therefore, we must be willing to sit down as citizens of the universe whose futures are clearly interwoven and interdependent and decide that either we hang together or we hang separately. Our love for God and for people should drive us to dialogue; our Biblical understanding should drive us to dialogue; our dispensational beliefs should bring us to dialogue. And, though we do not believe the same doctrines or live the same life-styles, we most certainly do have a deep common heritage in the Bible, the word of God.

If we cannot sit down together, it is unlikely that any two groups on Earth can. Ours would not necessarily be a spiritual fellowship but a religious dialogue for the purposes of guaranteeing to the children of Jews and Christians that there will be a next generation, and there will be a society of freedom out front for both of us. Finally, the fact that the basis of Judaism and Christianity is love—God's love toward us and our love toward Him and toward others—should cause us to remove the obstacles of the past and sit down and begin what we should have been doing for centuries.

Can you understand Jewish indifference and even hostility toward any attempt at Jewish-Christian rapprochement?

Yes, I can understand such indifference and hostility. Many Jewish individuals often confuse the attitudes and actions of the Gentile world at large with Christianity. This is a common, but serious mistake. Then again, within all the movements that go by the name of Christianity, there certainly are wide differences. Just because a Jim Jones *claimed* to have acted in the name of Christ doesn't make it so. I certainly hope there is no confusion about where I stand on these issues.

At the close of this part of our conversation, I asked Reverend Falwell to speak in general terms about the uniqueness of the Jewish people and how their religion has managed to survive.

The Jewish people, unlike any other family on Earth, was chosen by God to show His glory and to deliver His message to mankind. When one reads Genesis 11 and 12, it is very clear that God in His sovereignty selected Abram from Ur of the Chaldees to become the progenitor of a very special nation. In the New Testament, Romans chapters 9, 10, and 11 reaffirm God's commitment to the Jewish people.

The Jews are the chosen people of God. This statement infuriates some. There are those who would say this makes God to be a respecter of persons. I do not believe that. I believe that God, who is the creator and therefore the owner of all humanity and all things, has the right to do with the creation as He pleases. It has pleased God to select the Jewish people, out of no goodness of their own, based purely on His own sovereignty, to bear His glory and deliver His message.

He promised to this people a land. He promised to this special family His presence and His protection. Throughout the Old Testament, throughout the good and the bad days of Jewish history, He showed the surety of His word and the absoluteness of His promises repeatedly. The Jewish tradition has survived thousands of years of unbelievable persecution and submersion into the cultures of every age. Yet, after thousands of years of exile into practically all nations of the earth, the identity and the faith of the Jew has never been injured or obscured. This is not true of any other ethnic group on Earth. This survival is based upon nothing more or less than the keeping power of God and the surety of His promises.

Part Two

FALWELL ON
THE STATE
OF ISRAEL

2

Reverend Jerry Falwell's political support for the State of Israel has been widely publicized within the Jewish community during the last few years. Nevertheless, that support has been held suspect by the majority of Jews. His intentions have been consistently questioned and his motives impugned. It would be accurate to say that within the Jewish community Falwell's support for Israel has been rejected, ignored, or grudgingly accepted.

There exists a very wide gap between Falwell's consistently stated political positions on Israel and those which have been repeatedly presented to the public by the non-Jewish media—primarily, the popular daily press and the weekly news magazines—and the leaders of the liberal Christian community. A part of the problem lies within the Jewish community itself, a portion of which, even when aware of his stands on issues of interest to Jews, simply does not trust him. There is a feeling within their midst that he himself does not believe what he is saying, that his mouth is not in step with his heart. They tend to judge him not by his words and deeds, but by what they think lies in his subconscious.

The questions and answers in this chapter present Falwell's views on the State of Israel.

I began my conversation with Jerry Falwell on Israel by asking him to reminisce about his first trip to the Holy Land.

I made my first trip to Israel in the late 1960s. I had dreamed of such a trip for many years. I became a Christian as an 18-year-old college student and began reading the Bible extensively. The land of Israel became very enchanting to me because of the fact that Christianity had its beginnings there. I had read of all the Old and New Testament sites and of the happenings that occurred there. So, when I finally crossed the Allenby Bridge for the first time, coming from Amman, Jordan, toward Jerusalem, it was one of the most exciting days of my life. I well remember that day as we looked at the Jericho Road and travelled the highway up to Jerusalem from the Dead Sea area. I remember seeing the Bedouins in their tents as though it was 2,000 years ago; I remember passing Bethany, coming up over the Mount of Olives, and finally, for the first time ever, looking on the old city of Jerusalem. To describe my emotions would be impossible.

I suppose that all Christians have sensed this when they made their first trip to the Holy City. I would suspect that Jews from other lands have felt this same sensation. As I went from site to site rereading my Bible and the Biblical occurrences that transpired there, everything took on new meaning.

I suppose the most significant remembrance I have of my first visit to Jerusalem is how different is the land to the mental concept one gets from Bible study. I was shocked at how very small this little land really is. Suddenly, I began to realize that the most important piece of real estate in the world is also one of the tiniest.

The people, like the land, also made a great impression on me. The most impressive remembrance I have of the people is the kindness and courtesy they showed to Christian Americans who were making their first pilgrimage there. The patriotism of these people was astounding indeed. What had happened to their land in such a short time was amazing. As I visited town after town and went up and down the land of Israel, I marvelled at the commitment of the people to the rebuilding of their homeland. I imagined that our early American founding fathers must have had a similar commitment to carving a nation out of the wilderness and paying whatever price was necessary to do so. I left the land and the people of Israel with a greater commitment to the Bible, and a greater commitment to God's land and people.

I have visited Israel about a dozen times now. I never go there without experiencing the same sense of history and destiny. The novelty of visiting a Biblical or historical spot for the first time is no longer present, but I have never lost my wonder at the significance of this glorious place. It is my personal feeling that every Christian should set a personal life goal to visit Israel at least once. I know this is not possible for everyone. But I have never taken a tour group to Israel without feeling that, because of their visit, they will always be a friend to the people and the land.

For a Christian to have the all-consuming interest in Israel that you have is rare. Can you explain for us the source of this magnetism?

I feel that the destiny of the State of Israel is without question the most crucial international matter facing the world today. I believe that the people of Israel have not only a theological but also a historical and legal right to the land. I am personally a Zionist, having gained that perspective from my belief in Old Testament Scriptures. I have also visited Israel many times. I have arrived at the conclusion that unless the United States maintains its unswerving devotion to the State of Israel, the very survival of that nation is at stake. I think that the 1980s are going to be very critical times for Israel. Every American who agrees that Israel has the right to the land must be willing to exert all possible pressure on the powers that be to guarantee America's support of the State of Israel at this time.

When you say "the land," what precisely are you referring to? To Biblical Israel, from the Jordan to the Great Sea and from Mount Hermon to the Red Sea? From the Nile to the Euphrates? To pre-1967 Israel? To present-day Israel? What does a committed Christian see as the natural boundaries of the State of Israel?

Biblically, prophetically, and ultimately, "the land" will include that area promised to Abraham in Genesis 15:18. Even under Moses, Israel took possession of the entire East Bank, including most of that which is now ruled by Jordan (Numbers 32; Judges 11:13-26). Under the present realities, however, I am quite content to see Israel possess all the territory from the Jordan to the Mediterranean Sea. If Israel desires to give up part of her land to her neighbors, that is her business, but I do not favor that approach.

I believe there is a day coming when Israel will make a seven-year compact with a future world prince (Daniel 9:27). This coming world ruler will guarantee Israel's borders for a seven-year period, only to violate those borders himself after three and one-half years (Daniel 9:27; II Thessalonians 2:3-4; Matthew 24: 15-22). Israel's land will never be secure under this world's system. Only when the Messiah Himself rules will Israel dwell in peace (Zechariah 14:8-11).

Would it be wrong to say that your attraction to Israel is mainly theological?

I relate to the State of Israel in a threefold way. First, I relate in a humanitarian way. All earthly peoples have a Divine right to a land and a national purpose. The Jews are no exception. In fact, God gave them this land (Genesis 12:7; 15:18-21). Secondly, I relate in a political way. As a freedom-loving American, I am well aware that Israel is the sole democratic state in the Middle East, and the only real friend our country has there. Russia has made great inroads on occasion into practically every other nation over there except Israel. Thus, if for no other reason, I would be for strong support of Israel. Thirdly, I relate in a theological way. As has been previously stated, the basis of my theological support are the words found in Genesis 12:1-3.

You therefore see America's relationship with Israel as functioning on several levels? As more than just a vague moral commitment to Israel's survival?

The American commitment to Israel is based on moral, historical, and security considerations. Of course, America and Israel share common values and democratic traditions, but they also share a history of loving freedom and regarding liberty as an absolute necessity in a free society. So there is a great political affinity between the two allies. In addition, America sees Israel as a vital link in her international chain of security. Israel provides a source of strength in a vital geopolitical area and Israel is deeply interested in the free world's defense.

I personally believe that God deals with all nations in relation to how these nations deal with Israel. I think history supports this. I premise that on what God said to Abraham: "I will bless them that bless thee, and curse him that curseth thee" (Genesis 12:3). I therefore think America should without hesitation give total financial and military support to the State of Israel. My political support for Israel is unconditional.

You say that your political support of Israel is unconditional. Does that mean that Israel can do whatever it wants? Bomb nuclear reactors, invade foreign countries, occupy territories, all seemingly without any willingness to show flexibility, restraint, or compromise?

No, of course not. The bombing of the Iraqi nuclear reactor in the late spring of 1981 was totally justified. It was a defensive action. No one who knows the behavior and background of Saddam Hussein would suggest that Israel could take a chance on giving Iraq such an awful capability.

Nothing in the behavior of the government of the State of Israel—be it under the Labor Party or the Likud under Begin—would cause anyone to believe that Israel is irresponsible. Each of her wars has been fought out of necessity. The one thing that one must not lose sight of when referring to the Arab-Israeli conflict is that the Arabs have indicated time and again that, given the chance, they are determined to destroy the Jews . . . and not the other way around.

But isn't there a price limit on all of this? The United States will provide Israel with more than 3 billion dollars in aid in 1984. Given America's acute budgetary problems, does this make sense?

Israel is America's defense line in the Middle East. Israel is a proven military force, supreme in the area, and a bulwark in defending the Middle East against a Soviet-inspired communist takeover.

If the West had to maintain a force with equivalent capability in the area, it would cost many times what it costs her now and be not nearly as effective. Furthermore, the stationing of American troops in the area is a political impossibility since no Arab country has agreed to permit permanent American bases on its territory.

There are avowed friends of Israel who feel that American aid to Israel has a negative impact. They argue that it serves as a crutch. Instead of economic pressures forcing Israelis to increase their productivity, there is the knowledge that Uncle Sam will be around at the end of the year to balance the checkbook. Is it possible that the best favor the United States could do for Israel would be to reduce aid?

There is no question that it is in the best long-term interest of both Israel and the United States that Israel become self-sufficient. However, in the present reality, where even *with* American aid, the burden on the Israeli taxpayer to support a military establishment its size—the third largest air force in the world—is well beyond the carrying capacity of that country, maximum aid must continue to Israel. It must continue until the Israeli economy can expand enough to become self-sufficient.

Do you think the day will come when the American taxpayer will demand a drastic reduction in aid to Israel?

As long as the Soviet communist threat to the Middle East and the oil sources of the free world continues, it is hard for me to imagine that the American people will reach a conclusion that full American support of Israel is not in the best interests of the United States. Since its establishment in 1948, the American people have been very supportive of the survival and security of the State of Israel. And it is difficult for me to envision anything which would cause a fundamental change in this outlook.

From another perspective, is it not possible that beneath all the rhetoric and all the overt political jockeying the basic U. S.-Israeli relationship is a business relationship?

1. The United States supplies Israel with money and weapons, and Israel, in turn, relieves the United States of a policing function in a vital part of the world.

2. The United States supplies Israel with money and weapons, and Israel battle-tests those weapons, helps shake all of the bugs out of them with the aid of Israeli blood, and throws in access to one of the world's best intelligence organizations as a bonus.

This may be a *side-result* of the relationship; it is

certainly not the basis of the relationship. One would have to be completely cynical and utterly devoid of an historical feeling for the inseparable link between the United States and the State of Israel and its peoples to reach such a conclusion.

Does the fact that Israel is a religious state—a Jewish state—where religious law and secular law overlap disturb you?

No. Most nations of the world, except perhaps the communist/bloc, combine religious and secular concepts in their law systems. I believe the State of Israel is strengthened rather than weakened with such a state of affairs. The only disturbing element about it is the apparent lack of freedom for Christians to publicly proclaim their faith in Christ and to seek to practice their faith by sharing it with others.

How do you view the sale of AWACS electronic surveillance planes, as well as the F-15 enhancement package, to Saudi Arabia?

I think that it was a mistake. I felt it was an error originally when the Carter administration did what they did. I think enhancing the F-15 aggravates the problem. If in fact the real purpose for these jets was to prevent Soviet expansionism, that would be fine. But I have not yet heard any of the Saudis say that they support Israel's right to exist and will protect Israel's territorial rights. I think that in any Arab-Israeli conflict that might erupt there is the very definite danger that these planes may be used against the nation of Israel.

Since it is a 1985 delivery, I pray that something will happen between now and then to prevent the delivery from ever occurring. I can only say that the President feels really and truly committed to Israel. I do want to say this in defense of Mr. Reagan. He and I have different concepts on how to support that commitment. I don't feel that giving military arms to countries that are committed to the extinction of Israel is the way to do it.

There is no way to sit down at a negotiating table with murderers. That is exactly what Mr. Arafat and the PLO are all about; they are terrorists and murderers. There is no way to negotiate with heartless destroyers of men, women, and children such as the PLO. While I do not equate Arafat and the Saudi leaders, it is still dangerous for a country that is committed to the annihilation of Israel to be rewarded militarily; that is, by giving military help to them.

Is it possible to conceive of any situation in which the United States and Israel will suffer an irreconcilable falling out?

There will, of course, be areas of difference in specific instances, but in the overall framework, Israel and the United States share too many commonalities of values and traditions for there to be significant fundamental differences. Israel and the United States are committed to liberty, justice, and the preservation of democratic values in a world that is becoming increasingly totalitarian in nature.

Are Israel and America inextricably tied to each other? Do they share a common destiny?

One could justifiably answer this with a strong yes. That is to say, Israel and the United States share a common sense of what is necessary to protect freedom in this dangerous time. Israel needs and cherishes the support of the American government and a significant number of the American people. Israel looks to the United States for tangible aid and friendship. The United States sees Israel as the only freedom-loving, democratic nation in a sea of totalitarian states. The American government realizes that Israel can provide a vital service in protecting American interests in a crucial world area.

Israel is very much a part of the Free World. Her institutions are democratic in nature and indeed the West took its democratic political direction from the Hebrew Scripture. One might conclude that so long as the United States and Israel remain strong and free with a love of liberty they will remain viable nations. In a real sense, Israel and the United States are fighting on the front lines for democracy and freedom. They are engaged as partners against those nations who would destroy individual liberty and stamp out the Biblical values that have so enhanced freedom-loving societies.

Does a strong U.S.-Israeli relationship preclude an equally strong U.S.-Arab relationship?

The United States is interested in world peace and security. Thus, we are most concerned with establishing cordial relations with all nations that manifest a love of freedom. At the same time, we also seek to at least communicate with other nations, even those who are so different in political philosophy and approach. In recent years we have made a strong effort to communicate with the Arab nations and, I must say, that, with one or two exceptions, this communication has been a one-way street. *If* the Arab national interest is similar to ours, then by all means, we should understand their national interests. But they must make an equal effort to understand our interests. Israel is a vital part of our national interest. When the Arab nations digest this fact, instead of trying to wish it away, perhaps the first step in a mutual Arab-American relationship will have been taken.

Does the same potential bond exist between the Arab-Moslem nations and America as exists between Israel and America?

I would not say so. Of course, we seek peace in the Middle East as in all other world areas. We are working to achieve peace in the region and to bring the parties together. But let us remember that the history of relations between the United States and the Arab states is not very positive. Also, we cannot so closely link ourselves to nations who deny our basic way of life and who hold us in economic and political blackmail. Yes, we can have a relationship with the Arabs, one based on mutual need and respect. But, so long as these nations continue to accept totalitarian values and specifically refuse to recognize and deal with the reality of the nation of Israel, you might say that there is little basis for agreement on fundamental issues.

The United States was built on democratic principles. Our founding fathers were very much in touch with the Judeo-Christian tradition. The Arab-Moslem nations are alien to this tradition. I fail to see how we can share a common destiny with nations that aggressively seek to control other peoples and follow doctrines that foster territorial aggrandizement in the name of religion. Our destiny as a people is to support and enhance freedom for individuals and nations and to bring the principles of justice and morality into the human arena.

Moslems would take exception to what you say. They would argue that we all—Jews, Christians, Moslems—share a common heritage. They would point to Abraham, Isaac, and Jacob—all occupying prominent positions in the Koran. They would note the similarities between Jewish and Moslem dietary laws. They would stress the contributions Arabs have made to Western science, mathematics, and medicine. They would emphasize that Moslems have lived peacefully among Jews and Christians since the dawn of Islam. How would you answer them?

In Christ's Sermon on the Mount, He asserted that "ye shall know them by their fruits" (Matthew 7:16, 20). The seeming common heritage you have cited is only that of superficial appearance. Jews, Christians, and Moslems can also point back to Noah and even to Adam as a common ancestor, but that does not unite them in goal or purpose. Naturally, there are moderates in every camp, but the declarations of Arab summit leaders favor the destruction of the State of Israel. As a Christian, I am as much opposed to that Arab solution as I was to Hilter's "Final Solution."

In the eyes of the Arab-Moslem national entities, can there be a Moslem-Christian political coexistence any more than there can be a Moslem-Jewish political coexistence?

Yes, I am certain there can be temporary coexistence between Moslems and Christians, but when one examines the underlying Arab ideology and the historical reality one must conclude that that coexistence will only be transitory. American Christians must face the fact that the Moslem nations are motivated by a triumphalistic philosophy that wishes to regain lost territory and aggrandize new territory. In our time we have seen the use of oil as a blackmail weapon to achieve ends that endanger the West. In a utopian world everyone would have nothing to fear, but in this real world we must recognize the negative and dangerous tendencies of others. To do less would indicate an abdication of moral responsibility.

For a good part of this century, and especially for the last 30 years, the Arabs have been pursuing what has proven to be a very evasive pan-Arabism. The Arab nations like to see themselves as one unified world. The reality is otherwise: Lebanon, Syria, Egypt, Jordan, Iraq, and Libya have all been involved in wars and confrontations with brother Arab or Moslem countries in recent years. The one point around which they have consistently been able to rally has been Israel. Do you think that Arab hatred of Israel has persisted for so long because without it the Arab world would fall apart? Has it been a diversionary tactic to conceal Arab disunity?

The one area of agreement about which all Arab-

Moslem states rally is their enmity toward the Jewish State of Israel. There is no doubt that in the last decades the Arab position has congealed around an approach which precludes national rights for those who cannot be designated "Arab Moslems." The Christians in Lebanon, the Kurds in Iraq, and the Jews in Israel are ready examples. Because the Jews have been most successful in the achievement of national independence and sovereignty, they represent the greatest threat to the establishment of a solid block of Arab-Moslem states.

The inter-Arab struggle today contains a number of basic conflicts which have nothing to do with Israel:

1. Between Syria, on the one hand, and Jordan, Lebanon, and Israel on the other because Syria wishes to incorporate the latter countries into a Greater Syria in fulfillment of a historical national aspiration. The Syrian national constitution recognizes this.

2. Between Iraq and Syria over the water rights on their boundary.

3. Between the Saudis and the Gulf States with which they have border conflicts.

4. Between Libya and Egypt over Libya's perception of Egyptian wishes for her oil wealth.

5. Between Algeria and Morocco over the Sub-Sahara.

From all this, it is easy to see why the so-called Arab world is in perpetual turmoil. The only thing which holds it together is its hatred for Israel.

Do you think that the Arab leaders have been using hatred of Israel as a means of diverting the local population's attention from their, in some cases, hopeless economic situations?

Absolutely. Egypt has been perhaps the best example. With one of the lowest per capita incomes in the world, Egyptian leaders have always needed an external enemy in order to distract the public's attention from the terrible economic plight of that country. Even now, after Camp David, the impression that the controlled Egyptian press gives the local population regarding Israel is negative.

What do you see as a solution to the Palestinian Arab problem?

What to do with the so-called displaced Palestinians is a very difficult question to answer and a very real humanitarian problem. However, the State of Israel is such a tiny place geographically that no one could realistically expect Israel to give up a major part of her territory which is only about the size of New Jersey. I personally feel that the Arab nations need to sit down and, in a reasonable way, determine that they have a responsibility here. I am not anti-Arab. I am very much pro-human being. I think all sensible people are. But the problem in Israel is not one of skirmishes and battles and who wins today's conflict: it is a problem of survival. If a Palestinian state is in fact established on present Israeli soil, by someone such as

Arafat, I think the very existence of Israel will be challenged. Arafat has made it clear that his goal is the extinction of the State of Israel.

The number of Jewish and Arab refugees from the 1948 Arab-Israeli War is about equal: some 600,000 on each side. Israel successfully absorbed Jewish refugees from Arab countries; could not the Arab countries have absorbed the Arab refugees just as easily?

Without a doubt. The Arab refugees not only could have, but should have been absorbed long ago. The fact is that the refugees have not been allowed to join in with the citizens of the countries where they reside.

Why, then, have the Arabs been so interested in perpetuating the Palestinian problem? Is the "Palestinian problem" a myth?

The problem is not a myth, but it has been perpetuated by political decision. The problem could have been solved a generation ago by Arab absorption of their own people. But as a political football, the Palestinian people have been kicked around for a long time. Israel did not start the wars that created this problem. The Arabs began the wars and literally displaced their own peoples. Now it is their duty to make a home for them within their own borders.

It is no secret that many Palestinian refugees would be only too happy to take on the citizenship of the country in which they now reside, but are prohibited from doing so by their host countries. There are scores of cases in Southern Lebanon, for example, of Palestinians born in Lebanon 30 years ago to on Lebanese parent and one Palestinian refugee parent who are still labeled refugees and whose children, two-generations out of Palestine, are labeled refugees as well. Is there not some pressure the United States can put on Arab countries to grant full status to all its citizens? By funding organizations such as UNWRA, are we not helping to perpetuate the Palestinian problem?

I believe you are entirely right and I would like to see those precise changes come about.

Do you feel that the Pope's granting of an audience to Arafat enhanced the cause of peace?

I condemn in the strongest possible terms the Pope's reception of Arafat. I am at a loss to understand how this act could in any way enhance the possibilities of peace. On the other hand, I can see how this reception of the terrorist Arafat by a spiritual leader of the Pope's stature could encourage the forces of evil and darkness and make Arafat and his thugs as well as other terrorists feel their murderous acts will go uncondemned and unpunished. The reception of Arafat was a mistake that I fear will cause many innocent persons to pay dearly.

I admire the Pope's stand against the Soviets in the Polish situation. I appreciate his courageous stand on the moral and social issues. I am at a loss to understand why he met with Arafat.

Why do you think the Pope still refuses to recognize the State of Israel?

It is almost unbelievable that the Vatican still refuses to acknowledge the existence of the State of Israel. I fully understand the dilemma facing the Vatican with many Christians in Arab lands. However, it would seem that the same spirit of commitment to freedom that would cause the Pope to defy the Soviets in Poland would cause the Vatican to condemn those Arab nations that continue to hammer upon tiny Israel. It would appear that the same commitment to principle, to freedom, and to oppressed people would cause the Vatican to take a position on the side of a very definite underdog in the Middle East, Israel.

The Jerusalem Bill adopted by the Knesset formalized the status of Jerusalem as the legal capital of the State of Israel. The world didn't like this bill. How did you respond to it?

I think it was an excellent bill. I think it is ridiculous

that anyone would assume any other place to be the capital of Israel except Jerusalem.

My question to anyone who questions the status of the city of Jerusalem as the capital of Israel is: "Where is the capital of Israel?" Of course it's Jerusalem. Presently every Moslem, every Christian, every Jew can, for the first time in the many, many years I have been going to Israel, with the protection of the law, worship when, where, and how he pleases. I like that. That is the way we function here in America and the holy places of Jerusalem today are carefully protected again for the first time in a long time. Today the Moslem, Christian, and Jewish holy places have the full protection of the Israeli government. I think that's an excellent provision and I am hopeful that it is permanent.

And yet, there is hardly a foreign government which maintains an embassy in Jerusalem. Is this a healthy situation and can Israel do anything about it?

It is a disgusting situation, and I am sorry to admit that the U.S. embassy is located in Tel Aviv. I wish it were in Jerusalem as it should be. But this is a very politically-sensitive world in which we live. Israel could demand that all foreign embassies be moved to Jerusalem, but I am not certain that would bring about any great transformation. Too many nations want to remain as neutral and as uncommitted as possible.

Do you believe that Judea and Samaria should be part of the State of Israel?

There is no question that Judea and Samaria should be part of Israel.

At the time of the Camp David agreement, Sadat and Begin agreed on autonomy for the Arab residents of Judea and Samaria. It was further agreed that this autonomy would apply to populations and not to territories. Local Arabs would have control of local affairs—schools, health facilities, businesses—but not of Judea and Samaria as a united political entity. Arabs would not have control of area security, relations with foreign governments, water sources affecting the larger area. Do you think that this kind of autonomy, without promise of self-determination, will satisfy the Arabs of Judea and Samaria or will it forever be a point of contention?

The Camp David Accords were negotiated in good faith by men of goodwill. The courage of Sadat and Begin, with the support of President Carter, brought about the best agreement which could have been achieved given the conditions in the world in general and in the region in particular.

In a perfect world, there would be no minorities. Every group—thousands of them—would have its own country. In the real world, that is not possible. It is no more wrong for Arabs to live as a minority among

Jews than it was for Jews to live as a minority among Arabs—as was the case for generations. In time, I hope that the Arabs of Judea and Samaria will come to recognize this as have countless other minorities. There is no other choice.

There seem to be two practical possibilities for the eventual status of Judea and Samaria: (1) the autonomy just described and (2) annexation with full Israeli citizenship for all Arabs who wish it. Which alternative do you think would be most democratic? Which do you think would be best for Israel?

Israel must maintain control over all the land west of the Jordan River to meet her future security needs. The government of Israel as represented by its people will have to decide what is best. It is a democratic society and the final decision will be as a result of the democratic process within Israel.

Do you believe the Reagan plan for Jordanian control of the West Bank to be correct and workable?

The Reagan Plan of 1982 is the Rogers Plan of the late 1960s under a new name. It troubles me that this administration went beyond the Camp David Accords to which the United States is a signatory. Let us recall that Jordan did indeed control the so-called West Bank from 1948 to 1967. Yet she did not set up an independent Palestinian state during those years, nor did she make any special effort to satisfy what we have come to know in the 1980s as Palestinian "rights." The West Bank, more properly known as Judea and Samaria, is the heartland of the Jewish Biblical and historical patrimony and, as such, the eternal possession of the Jewish people. I have visited this area many times and from the security point of view I would not like Jordan, a nation that continues to refuse to recognize Israel's right to exist, to control it or pass control over to another hostile force which would dominate the high ground overlooking the population center of Israel.

Do you believe that the Reagan Plan is in America's best interest?

I am convinced that the President is concerned with developing a foreign policy that is in America's best interest. He is committed to America's security and the security of the free world. Unfortunately, I do not see his Middle East peace plan as serving the interests of American security. The plan is unworkable, violates the Camp David Accords, and assumes that the PLO—a terrorist, outlaw band—would be willing to coexist with the Jewish state, a state they have sworn to destroy in their national covenant. I believe that the President should encourage direct face-to-face negotiations between Israel and her neighbors without preconditions. Let us go back to the spirit that brought Sadat and Begin to the negotiating table rather than working out the details of a settlement before the parties have even agreed to talk

Let's consider a hypothetical question. Let's say that sometime within the next year Jordan and/or Syria reverse themselves and not only openly avow Israel's right to exist, but (with or without honest intent) also agree to sit down and negotiate with Israel. Would such a situation compel Israel to return the Golan Heights, East Jerusalem, and Judea and Samaria to their pre-1967 administrators, or even in such a situation would Israel, by virtue of its historical claims as well as its investment since 1967, be morally free to do as it sees fit with these lands?

Even in such a farfetched situation, the threat against Israel will persist because the Arab countries are dictatorships, not democracies. As quickly as their leaders change, so can their policies. Arab leaders in fact have a history of breaking agreements. The territory of Israel is too small and too vital to its security to trust the ephemeral goodwill of Arab leaders.

Do you think that the larger world grasps the extent of the Israeli government's commitment to the Jewish settlement of Judea and Samaria? Towns and cities are literally springing up in the night—there will soon be 100,000 Jews living in the area—and yet the American government and others continue to talk as if eventually and inevitably these settlements will be removed. Why do you think this is?

The Western world—including the United States —has accepted the so-called moderate Arab approach to what Israel's borders should be. Basically, this implies a return to the pre-1967 situation. But Israel hasn't accepted this view and it doesn't appear that it will. Today, there is massive settlement in Judea and Samaria. If the Israelis are determined to hold these territories, in time the world will come to accept it.

Israel has annexed the Golan Heights. What is your position on this matter?

I believe that the Golan Heights should be an integral part of the State of Israel.

Israel's invasion of Lebanon in June 1982 achieved historical results. It succeeded in destroying a terrorist fighting force (the PLO) and putting an end to an unwanted seven-year domination by a foreign army (the Syrians). And yet the world has all but forgotten both the intent and the achievement of the Israeli action. Put the Israeli achievement in a historical perspective for us and explain to us why the world has reacted the way it has.

The world is myopic because of the importance of Arab oil to the Western industrialized economy and the influence of recycled Arab money on Western society. In other words, the Western position is based on perceived self-interest rather than on principle.

The destruction of the PLO as a fighting force and its expulsion from Beirut as well as the neutralization of Syrian forces in Western and Southern Lebanon was a terrible blow to the Soviet Union. The most sophisticated terrorist force in the history of mankind was brought to its knees. Had they been allowed to build up in Lebanon much longer, there is no question that the Syrians and PLO would have been a grave danger to Northern Israel.

What do you see as the eventual status of Lebanon?

Lebanon must be a free and independent nation outside the control and domination of foreign forces. This nation has suffered under outside control and influence whether we talk of Syrian rule or PLO terrorist rule. It is time for Lebanon to return to her former role as a democratic, freedom-loving nation. Israel's "Peace for Galilee" campaign set in motion the process by which this happy goal may be achieved.

How do you explain the hysterical reaction by the Free World press, its leaders, and institutions against Israel to the massacre of 700 to 800 Palestinians by the Christian Phalangists which occurred at the Sabra and Shatila refugee camps outside Beirut in September 1982?

The media in a sense lies in wait for Israel. Every Israeli action is examined more carefully than the activities of almost any other nation. More often than not, and usually without cause, Israel is found wanting by the media. I wonder if that is the price Israel must pay for being a free society and allowing the media access to its military, political leadership, and inhabitants. The media reaction after the massacre was unjustified and proved again how biased and self-righteous the media can be.

Is this reaction evidence that Israel and the Jewish people are being subjected to a double standard?

There is no question that the media displays a double standard in reporting on Israel. I can think of few nations who receive a more biased treatment from the media than Israel. Of course we know that the PLO intimidated Western correspondents in Lebanon for years and that may be part of the story. Arafat, the terrorist murderer, is a media hero while Begin, the democratically elected leader of a free people, is a media scapegoat. The media must clean up its act and perhaps it is time for fair-minded media consumers to make known their displeasure at Israel's treatment.

Do you see a tendency toward support of Israel in the Christian Community?

In the past twenty years, Fundamentalists and Evangelicals, at a very rapid pace, have been "converting" to support for Israel. This has not been a traditional position. It is a position taken today by the majority of Evangelicals and Fundamentalists in this country. Leading pastors and preachers across the nation have begun taking a very courageous stand on what they have always believed theologically but have never been willing to take a stand on practically. With every passing day, the number of supporters of Israel is outdistancing those that oppose Israel in the Evangelical-Christian community. It is my feeling that the best friends Israel has in the world today are among Evangelical and Fundamentalist Christians. I think five years from now that consensus will be virtually unanimous.

And yet, while the Evangelical Church has strengthened its ties with Israel, the Liberal Church has taken an opposite stand. Why is this?

It is very significant, probably the most significant happening in the Jewish-Christian relationship ever, that at this point in history, Conservative Christians—what some would call rightist—are rapidly becoming committed friends of the Jews and of Israel. At the same time, the Liberal Church—some would say leftist—traditionally a friend of the Jew, is repudiating that friendship. The World Council of Churches and its American version—the National Council of Churches has, and I don't know the reasons why, in recent years become more and more committed to the Marxist-Leninist philosophy. That commitment to Marxism has manifested itself in many ways—and the CBS program "60 minutes" recently exposed this organization's financial support of many Marxist governments and guerrilla groups, including the PLO, worldwide. With that commitment to Marxist-Leninism has come a cooling of its relationship with Israel.

There is no question that the Arab states have aligned themselves with the Soviet Union and the World Council of Churches. Again, I don't understand why. The World Council of Churches has come to believe that the so-called liberation fighters, like the PLO, around the world—I call them guerrillas, murderers, terrorists—are really the champions of freedom in today's world. It increasingly looks on the United States and Israel as enemies to the true cause of world peace. For that reason, the Jew and the State of Israel find themselves in quite a dilemma. Their perennial friends at the WCC talk friendship but abort long-standing agreements with Israel. At the present moment, most Jews look on the World Council of Churches as the enemy camp. The so-called liberation theology of the liberal churchmen in many parts of the world is nothing more than an accommodation of Marxism—and an encouragement to bloody revolution on the part of radical terrorist groups. The liberation theologians almost always oppose democratic governments like the United States and Israel.

What is the World Council of Churches and who are its members?

The world Council of Churches is an umbrella organization. It has scores of denominations. The United Methodist Church, several of the Presbyterian and Episcopalian Churches, some of the Baptist groups, the United Church of Christ, and others belong. The Roman Catholic Church and the Southern Baptist Convention are two large denominations that do not hold membership. It is not Evangelical; it is not Fundamentalist. Its attitude toward Israel would be similar to its attitude toward the Fundamentalist-Evangelical Church. Fortunately, these liberal churches are diminishing in numbers and finances. The American people are turning from these churches and, as George Gallup said recently, the most dynamic phenomenon in America today is the growth of those churches which hold to orthodox religion, particularly Fundamentalist-Evangelical Christianity.

The Executive Body of the Presbyterian Church, which represents its two-and-a-half million members, called for an American cut-off of aid and an embargo in arms shipments to Israel as a response to the Beirut Massacre. How do you explain this?

Well, this is the same group that gave ten thousand dollars to Angela Davis at the height of her prominence. Frankly, I am not surprised at anything this body does. We know that the WCC [World Council of Churches] has been supportive of terrorism in Africa and other regions, and that the WCC has generally followed a pro-Arab position in recent years. The United Presbyterian Church should more carefully examine its role in public affairs and refrain from such one-way non-contributive statements. Fortunately, the American people recognize the Presbyterian action as just empty rhetoric and reject this attempt to harass and weaken our ally Israel.

Do you believe Israel as a nation should be judged in its political and military behavior by higher standards of conduct and morality than the Christian democratic nations of the West?

Of course not. All nations should be treated on an equitable basis with regard to the morality of their policies and actions. Israel, if anything, should be judged as having acted in the most favorable ethical and moral light in her 35-year history as a free and independent nation. Few nations could withstand the moral scrutiny Israel has faced. Israel must act in accordance with her security requirements and must keep in mind the needs of her people. No other nation, and certainly not a biased world press, can tell Israel how to act or can stand in overarching moral judgment over Israel's actions.

And yet, perhaps it is Israel's function and fate to be scrutinized by godly standards. For, as the Scriptures say, Israel is to be "a beacon to the heathens" (Isaiah 42:6).

I would not say it is the Israelis' *function* to be scrutinized this way. As to their fate, it would be more accurate to say that as God's chosen people they are the object of Satan's hatred. Therefore, it is naturally expected that they will be scrutinized and criticized in this fashion.

When it took power in November 1980, the Reagan Administration adopted the security of the Persian Gulf as its prime foreign policy target. Why do you believe it has now shifted emphasis from the Gulf to the Palestinian issue?

I find this difficult to understand. In this topsy-turvy world, everything seems to hinge on the so-called Palestinian problem. Of course, the Palestinians are entitled to justice and, of course, their problems must be ameliorated, but not at the expense of other more vexing and potentially dangerous problems. The Palestinian issue is much more complex than the media and State Department Arabists would like us to believe. American preoccupation with the Palestinians will inhibit the possibility of a just solution and will divert our attention away from vital problems crying for solution. I am greatly concerned with the Iran-Iraq War and the security of the Persian Gulf. Yet, in the mind of the Administration, this major issue takes a back seat to the Palestinians. Why not let the autonomy provisions of Camp David have a chance for success and let Israel, Egypt, and those Palestinians not under PLO domination or intimidation work out a solution?

How do you think Saudi Arabia influences American foreign policy?

The Saudis have oil reserves and they have also made considerable economic investment in American institutions. They also exercise significant influence over other Arab nations. In a sense, they are a pivot upon which the United States has attempted to build a policy of positive relationship with the Arab world. The problem is that the Arab world is diverse and lacking unity. My own sense is that we have been too susceptible to Saudi pressure without seeking adequate quid pro quo. We must ask the Saudis to talk sense to those Arabs they influence—particularly with reference to Israel's right to exist and her security requirements. The Saudis must perceive us to have resolve and determination and, if needed, the will to resist blackmail and boycott.

Logically, as the world oil market continues to soften, Saudi influence should abate. Do you think Americans with economic interests in the Arab world will "allow" Saudi influence to fall to "market levels"?

It is doubtful. Most American economists, industrialists, and politicians have an inflated perception of the importance of Saudi oil to our domestic health. There is very little commitment to doing what is necessary in order to become self-sufficient as far as energy is concerned.

Prior to the fall of the Shah of Iran, the American press and government were extremely critical of the corruption, lack of democratic institutions, and lack of human rights in Iran. Why has the American press or the American government never exhibited a similar sensitivity to seemingly parallel conditions in Saudi Arabia and the Gulf States?

We treat Saudi society with great reserve and caution. This may be due to foreign policy concerns and to the demands of American businessmen active in the Saudi marketplace. Of course, the Iranian situation was highly dramatic and extreme. The Shah also allowed the American press remarkable access.

I have little doubt that many negative factors are at work in Saudi Arabia, but on a less visible level. Western attempts to expose undemocratic activities in Saudi Arabia or to criticize governmental practice have met with strong resistance and the threat of economic countermeasures. So long as we remain frightened by the actions of a totalitarian regime, we will lack the will to condemn the undemocratic facets of Saudi life.

Is it possible that Arab influence in the State Department and the press tilted policy against the Shah, America's number one ally in the Gulf?

The Shah was extremely unpopular with some segments of the media though I happen to recall that some journalists, who later became his hostile critics, enjoyed his lavish hospitality in the early 1970s. The Shah had many failings, but he did provide stability at home, and he was a strong friend of America. In any case, we see what has happened to Iran since the Shah's downfall. I wouldn't imagine that even the Shah's strongest critics would have wanted events to transpire in the way they have. This is a lesson for us. In setting up the conditions for the overthrow of one leader disliked by politicians and reporters, we may set in motion the seeds of evils unimagined in previous regimes.

How do you explain the sharp increase in anti-semitism and anti-Israel manifestations over the last number of years?

If you make Israel the enemy, if you fail to condemn terrorism, if you give in to blackmail, if you put all of the responsibility for settlement of the Middle East problem on Israel, then you create an atmosphere in which anti-Semitism can flourish. Every Christian must join in the struggle against this age-old scourge. No Christian can be anti-Semitic and indeed all Christians must join in the battle against all manifestations of anti-Jewish activity in every part of the world. My organization, Moral Majority, has as one of its foundational precepts the protection of the rights of Jews everywhere. In my view, one of the great antidotes to the poison of anti-Semitism is the concern and activities of Bible-believing Christians who love and respect the Jewish people and stand fully for Israel's just cause.

Do you believe anti-Semitism would disappear if Israel were to submit to all of America's political wishes?

No, anti-Semitism will continue until individuals recognize its pathological nature and inherent evil. Israel cannot be lulled into thinking that capitulation to policies it knows endanger its survival will result in an outpouring of love and support from the outside world. Israel must act out of her security needs and her requirements as a free, sovereign nation. American Christians will support Israel and will fight any manifestation of anti-Semitism.

Is a militarily strong, free, and democratic Jewish nation in the Middle East really in the best interests of the United States and the Free World given the Arab-Moslem world's fundamental opposition to such an entity?

America must have a global strategy in these crisis-ridden days. This strategy must find strong links in the overall chain. Israel is without doubt one of these links. We must have a reliable ally in the Middle East. The fall of Iran, the weakness of Jordan, the economic threats of the Saudis, and the increase of Soviet influence in this crucial world arena demand a viable, secure American friend. We must do everything possible to aid Israel and to enhance her defense and security positions. A strong independent Israel helps the Free World and also provides an ideological base for democracy—that shrinking commodity in the increasingly totalitarian world of the late 20th century. We must never allow the enmity of the Arab world toward Israel to weaken our resolve or deter our course of helping Israel remain free, strong, and independent.

If Israel did not exist would there be peace in the Middle East, oil flowing at reasonable prices, no Arab refugees, and an Arab-Moslem world united with the West against world communism?

Of course not. On the contrary, there would be more friction and a greater threat to Western and Free World security. If there were no Israel, the Arab states would continue to act out of their self-interest. They would squeeze the West economically and politically, and they would provide the basis of instability so hospitable to Soviet penetration and domination. The Arab refugee problem was a creation of the Arab nations and continues to this day largely as a result of Arab policy. There is no present indication that the Arab nations would fight communism and join with the Free World. Above all, the underlying Moslem ideology would keep the Arab states and the West on a confrontation course. Indeed a strong viable Israel is the best deterrent to the realization of Arab-Moslem dreams of aggrandizement.

At the close of our conversation on Israel, I asked Reverend Falwell to talk about the link between Christianity and a reborn Jewish state.

Anyone who truly believes in the Bible sees Christianity and the new State of Israel as inseparably connected. The reformation of the State of Israel in 1948 is, for every Bible-believing Christian, a fulfillment of Old Testament and New Testament prophecy. Jesus predicted the "Budding of the Fig Tree." We believe the fig tree is Israel. We believe that God, in fulfillment of the prophecies of Deuteronomy and the other passages, has regathered his people from all corners of the earth to this very place that God promised to Abraham thousands of years ago.

When God established the boundaries of Israel in Genesis 15, He was very explicit. Because we are Bible-believing Christians, we know that no word of prophecy can ever be broken. As Christians we also believe in the Abrahamic Covenant, which in essence states that God deals with nations in relation to how nations deal with Israel. It is my feeling that every American Christian should be exerting all influence available to him in guaranteeing that his government is ever in total support of this land of Israel, this state that has miraculously evolved before our very eyes.

Part Three

FALWELL ON CONTEMPORARY MORAL ISSUES AND ON HIS MINISTRY

3

The problem that many Jews have in accepting
Jerry Falwell's support of Israel derives directly from
his position on contemporary moral issues. For many
decades now, Jews have been heavily identified with
the liberal spectrum of American life. Wherever liberal
causes have been found, Jews have been active in great
numbers: in the civil rights movement, in the women's
movement, in the labor movement. Their progressive
outlook is dear to Jews, many of whom see it as a
natural extension of their ancient religious heritage.

This being the case, it is not surprising that Jews
would have trouble identifying with Jerry Falwell.
Falwell is a traditionalist; he believes that people who
live without religion lead incomplete lives. He believes
that abortion is alien to a love and respect for life. He
believes that homosexuality is a perversion which
should not be accepted as an alternate life-style. These
are his positions. But, to be satisfied with labeling
Falwell as an arch-conservative, and to thus conclude

that he has nothing in common with Jews, does an injustice to both the perceiver and the perceived.

Understanding Falwell requires first of all an appreciation that he plies two paths: as a spiritual leader who touches tens of millions of Americans and as a political force speaking out to the nation on the most controversial issues of the day. It also requires an appreciation of his background: as a Southerner raised in a rural atmosphere at a time when to call a black man a "nigger" was accepted practice and when to envision a Jew was to see a man with horns and tails. But, most important, it requires an appreciation that, like other leaders, Falwell's views have undergone drastic—almost revolutionary—changes since his formative years.

The questions and answers in this chapter present Falwell's views on contemporary moral issues and on his ministry.

I began this part of my conversation with Jerry Falwell by asking him to assess the changes which have taken place in the moral climate of the country over the last few decades.

America's parents came out of World War II in 1945 having experienced the worst economic depression and the worst war in our nation's history. These parents were determined that their children would never experience the awful things they had faced: determined that their children would never be deprived of the things which they had not possessed. And thus America's parents—you and I—gave "things" to their children. We gave them automobiles: we gave them money: we gave them the educational privileges we had never had.

But in giving these "things" to our children, we

failed to simultaneously communicate to them the principles and the value system which makes "things" meaningful. We, therefore, ushered in a period of unprecedented materialism. In the mid-1950s this materialism began to fail our young people. A period of rebellion was initiated. The rock music culture and drug culture came along about the same time. Our sons and daughters began to rebel against the "establishment." They turned against their parents. They turned against their government and flag. They burned their campuses. They rejected the traditional family and began a period of moral permissiveness. Live-in arrangements became prevalent.

The 1960s and 1970s became two decades of moral and spiritual decadence. Pornography exploded everywhere. The homosexual revolution had its birth. A 40 percent divorce rate developed. Secular humanism became the prominent philosophy of the day. The free enterprise system became an object of hate and distrust. Business became "bad." Government was looked on as corrupt and exploitative. In other words, America almost ceased to be America.

Nowhere was this deterioration more obvious than in the areas of education. Young people graduated from high school unable to read or write. Our colleges no longer produced young people with leadership ability. Other nations of the world began to outstrip the U.S. in every area. To compound our problems, 20 million Americans were found to have Herpes as a result of promiscuous heterosexual behavior. Other venereal diseases became rampant. And then came AIDS.

But somewhere in the mid-1970s, according to all the pollsters, there began an awakening process among our young people. Our youth began to realize that they had been victims of a very bad social experiment during the previous decades. They had been exploited by social engineers and secular humanists. And with this awakening came a repudiation. According to Gallup and Harris, young people began to return to the moral values of their grandparents. It is now generally accepted that young people are more conservative than their parents. Most of the major news magazines are now recognizing that traditional values are back in. Marriage is now looked on as important. Church weddings are again prevalent. According to Gallup, 41 percent of America's young people are now reading the Bible (compared with 27 percent in 1978). According to Gallup our young people are returning to the basics of the Judeo-Christian tradition on which this nation was founded.

There is much yet to be accomplished. At the present moment, America is aborting nearly two million babies annually. Over 13 million unborn babies have been destroyed in this nation since the Roe vs. Wade Supreme Court ruling of January 1973 legalizing abortion on demand. Infanticide is practiced widely. Euthanasia is not that far down the road.

Fortunately, as I see it, the nation is making a turn to the right on most of the traditional values and moral issues which are vital to our nation's survival. I am optimistic that historians will record the 1980s as a decade of moral and spiritual rebirth in this country.

Your path to the Church was not paved by your early years. How did you first become involved in religion?

My father never attended church in his life. His father before him professed to be an atheist. I was converted to Jesus Christ as a result of hearing a radio broadcast which originated from the Long Beach Municipal Auditorium in Long Beach, California. Dr. Charles E. Fuller was the speaker on this broadcast. During my high school years and my first two years of college, I listened regularly to Dr. Fuller each Sunday morning. My mother, who was a Christian, would leave the radio playing on Sunday morning as she went off to church so that I could hear the simple message of the Gospel of Jesus Christ from Dr. Fuller. In the meantime, I became aware of my personal need to embrace the Lord Jesus Christ as my Savior.

In January of 1952, I began looking for a Church which preached the same message as Dr. Fuller. On Sunday night, January 20, 1952, I walked inside the little Park Avenue Baptist Church in Lynchburg, Virginia, with a determined purpose to become a Christian. I publicly acknowledged Jesus Christ as my Lord and Savior at the conclusion of that service. I purchased my first copy of the Scriptures the next morning. I joined that Church and was later baptized there.

At that time, I was in my second year of studies at Lynchburg College. I was studying pre-mechanical engineering. Since I had very little spiritual and religious background, this was a dramatic and new beginning for me. I began studying the Bible regularly. My deep involvement with the ministry of the Park Avenue Baptist Church was a great help to me in my spiritual development. In the fall of 1952, having felt that God was calling me into full-time Christian ministry, I enrolled at Baptist Bible College in Springfield, Missouri. Four years later, I returned to my hometown, Lynchburg, Virginia, and founded the Thomas Road Baptist Church with 35 charter members. I have pastored this church since that time. We now have more than 20,000 members—and church membership continues to grow rapidly.

Many American Jews have become paranoid about the Moral Majority. They simply can't perceive of an evangelical organization as bringing any good to American Jews. Tell us first what the Moral Majority is and how it fits into the religious and political stream of the country.

The Moral Majority is not an evangelical organization. It is not a religious organization. It is a political coalition of Americans from every religious persuasion now numbering approximately 6½ million who agree on several moral positions. Membership in the Moral Majority can be obtained by any American who is pro-life, pro-traditional family, pro-moral, and pro-American. Under those last two tenets, we have several emphases. Under the pro-moral tenet, the Moral Majority takes a strong position against the illegal drug traffic in this nation, against pornography, against homosexuality (but not against homosexuals). Under the pro-American tenet, the Moral Majority takes a stand in support of strong national defense and unswerving support for the State of Israel. We feel that these are indeed moral issues.

No one disputes the fact that drugs, pornography, homosexuality, and abortion are moral issues. However, some will argue that national defense is not a moral issue. In my opinion they are wrong. I feel that the basic moral issue of all moral issues is freedom. Not one person in Afghanistan is discussing pornography or abortion today. The primary issue there is survival.

We cannot adequately guarantee peace and freedom to our children unless we are stronger than the hostile aggressor, which happens to be the Soviet Union. History has proven that the intentions of the Soviets are not good. They are committed to world conquest.

I think it is in the particular interest of America to be supportive of the State of Israel, its only true friend in the Middle East. If we were to withdraw our support of Israel, there is very little, humanly speaking, to prevent the enemies of Israel from driving her into the Mediterranean Sea.

The Moral Majority is committed to these particular issues. We have Jewish members; we have Roman Catholic members; we have Mormons, Protestants, and Fundamentalists. All that is necessary for membership in Moral Majority is American citizenship and a commitment to the aforementioned shared moral values.

You say you have Jewish members. Would, for example, an American Zionist, a member of an Orthodox Jewish Synagogue, a member of the board of an Orthodox Hebrew day school be eligible to be a member of the Moral Majority?

He most certainly would be. We are hopeful of attracting a very large constituency of Jewish people in the Moral Majority during the 1980s. I personally feel that Bible-believing conservative Christians and conservative, traditional Jews are either going to stand together or we are going to fall together. I feel we need to move quickly, as never before, to merge conservative Christian America with conservative, traditional Judaism in those political causes that involve freedom and liberty.

Can one maintain his Jewish beliefs and identity, without embracing Christ, and still be involved in the Moral Majority and with your cause?

Yes. As a matter of fact you can belong to Moral Majority as an atheist. I don't believe we have any atheists involved in Moral Majority. However, it is conceivable that an atheist could be pro-life, pro-family, pro-moral, pro-Israel, and pro-strong national defense without believing in God. It is unlikely, but conceivable. What I am saying is this: Any American can belong to Moral Majority as long as he or she is committed to our shared moral values.

How do you raise your funds?

The millions of Moral Majority members contribute voluntarily. We have no membership dues. The national Moral Majority organization has a budget of $12 million this year. Each of the state chapters has its own budget and must raise its own funds. It is always on a free-will contribution basis.

We have recently set a goal to double membership in the Moral Majority during the next 12 months. We are experiencing our most rapid growth at this time.

You say that the Moral Majority is a political movement. Is that correct?

That is correct.

When did the Moral Majority first officially announce that it was a political organization?

The national Moral Majority, of which I am President, is headquartered in Washington, D.C. We officially organized in June 1979, and announced that we were a political organization at that time. There are 50 state chapters. Each of these state chapters is indigenous and autonomous. Some of them have political action committees; some do not. Some endorse candidates; some do not. Some get involved in local issues which are not of interest to the national organization.

Exactly how are the 50 state-level Moral Majority chapters organized and what is their relationship to the national Moral Majority?

The national Moral Majority has allowed 50 state chapters—one per state—to use the name Moral Majority, Inc. They sign a declaration stating that the day they cease to believe in the political doctrinal positions of Moral Majority, they will surrender the name. That is all there is to it. We have no franchises. Every state chapter has its own board of directors, its corporation, and its own local focus. Each uses the methodology which best suits its point of view. Each chapter is autonomous.

These state chapters generally look to national headquarters for advice and direction. But they are not controlled by the national office. As a result, from time to time, there have been strange and unfortunate pronouncements made that do not represent the view of the national Moral Majority.

The breakdown in function between the national Moral Majority and the state chapters is still not clear. On the one hand, according to the way you describe it, there doesn't seem to be any coordination between state and national levels. On the other hand, the national organization seems to do all the glamorous and important work, leaving little purpose for the state organizations.

It is true that the national Moral Majority develops policy and makes most of the national pronouncements. It is also true that the national Moral Majority exercises philosophical control over the state organizations through voluntary interaction.

Our national newspaper, the *Moral Majority Report*, is published, edited, and printed by the national Moral Majority. Most of the state chapters receive regular communications from the national office as to the issues and battles in which we are engaged. By telephone and letter, our state co-laborers receive weekly direction from us.

However, as I have previously stated, the state chapters are not franchises or subsidiaries of the national office. Each state chapter has its own board of directors. It is individually chartered in its respective state. The use of the name—Moral Majority, Inc.— gives us the right to demand that the state chapters never deviate from the doctrinal positions of the national Moral Majority. But again, each state chapter must raise its own funds and develop its own programs. We have come to the conclusion that this kind of loose arrangement is better than other possible alternatives.

A while back, one of the members of a Moral Majority chapter, appearing on the "Good Morning America" television show, displayed a Bible on his knee, pointed to the Bible and said, "This country was based and built on this Bible." Doesn't the above cast a shadow on your professed separatism of church and state?

I didn't see that program. However, I would see nothing wrong with the interviewer or the interviewee having a Bible on the program and commenting from it. There is a Bible on the podium in the United States Congress. Many civic clubs in America open with a prayer and a reading from the Old Testament or New Testament. This kind of activity does not make the Congress a religious organization. Nor do civic clubs become religious because they may open with a prayer. The Presidential inauguration always involves a prayer. That does not make the inauguration a religious event.

You claim very strongly that you adhere to the separation of church and state. And yet you seem to favor legislation that would allow "scientific creationism"—the view that God created the world—to be taught in public schools.

My desire to have evolution and "scientific creationism" taught in public schools alongside each other is a question of academic freedom. These are the two dominant philosophies of origin which are competing in American academia today. There are those who believe in Darwinian evolution. According to most of the major pollsters, an even larger number of Americans believe in special and divine creation. I am simply asking that, in the name of academic freedom, both philosophies be presented in America's classrooms. As I see it, nothing is to be lost or endangered when all facets of truth and information are presented to young people.

At Liberty Baptist College, where I am Chancellor,

we present both philosophies to our young people. In chapel programs, I declare our belief in special creation. Biology instructors teach science in the classroom. Our students are then allowed to make up their own mind regarding the origin of species. Our biology graduates have been tested academically on national tests and compared with biology graduates from colleges across the country they have done well. They are in the 75 percentile. This means they are doing better than 75 percent of the biology graduates nationwide. We would like to see the strong support for academic freedom demonstrated here at Liberty practiced everywhere.

There is a widely held impression in the street that your goal is to Christianize America. Do you see a viable American Jewish community in the America of the future?

It is as ridiculous to assume that America can be Christianized as to believe that it can be Judaized. The distinctiveness of America is the fact that we are a melting pot for the peoples of the world. While America is predominantly Judeo-Christian, there is also room for the Moslem. There is room for the Hindu. There is room for the atheist.

As a born-again Christian, I obviously believe that the great commission to the Christian Church is to evangelize the world. I believe in my heart that I have a responsibility to attempt to share the Gospel of Jesus Christ with every person in my generation. However, there is no Biblical basis for believing that the majority of the population of this nation or any nation at any time in history will ever be Christian. The results are left up to God.

The American Jewish community in the America of the future will be a very strong and prosperous one. A truly Christian environment is an environment of love and tolerance. There are distortions and aberrations of Christianity which history reports. We look back at the Crusades. We read of the various cults and of the Jim Jones tragedy. But this is not true Biblical Christianity.

But, if you say that you don't want to Christianize America, why then do you need a Christian "Bill of Rights"?

Let me start off by stating that the Christian Bill of Rights was an Old-Time Gospel Hour-Thomas Road Baptist Church presentation of our religious views. It was in no way connected with the Moral Majority and does not in any way allege that we have any interest in "Christianizing" America.

The Christian Bill of Rights started as a full-page ad which ran in *TV Guide* and a number of other magazines several years ago. In that Christian Bill of Rights, we shared our desire to see America return to the traditional and moral values on which the nation was established. In that newspaper ad, we addressed the issue of abortion. We addressed pornography, homosexuality, the 40 percent divorce rate, and the traditional family. The Christian Bill of Rights was never intended to be a legislative matter. We were simply saying that we would like to see America return to those traditional values which we have held for so many years.

It has never been our intention that the Christian Bill of Rights, as we published them, be incorporated into national or state law. We never wanted to use these tenets to become a part of our legislative or judicial system. It was simply a statement of our philosophy and our convictions. If we were to launch out into a similar endeavor in the future, we would call it the "Judeo-Christian Bill of Rights." This would not provoke the criticism that our previous effort caused.

It is my conviction that this nation was built upon the Judeo-Christian ethic. When I use the term "Judeo-Christian" I refer to the principles of the Old Testament (Judeo) and the principles of the New Testament (Christian).

The Judeo-Christian ethic is the cornerstone of our republic and contains seven basic principles. (See page 118.)

I strongly believe in the separation of church and state. I do not believe in the separation of God and state. The First Amendment protects churches from the government.

In America today, 96 percent of all Americans profess to be theists. I do not wish to exclude those 4 percent of unbelievers from first class citizenship rights. At the same time, I do not want to see the 96 percent of believers to be discriminated against. I personally believe we have done that during the past 25 years in this country. The American Civil Liberties Union, in my opinion, and other such organizations, have almost made it unpopular and undesirable to be religious. I certainly want to reverse that trend in our nation.

	Judeo Ethic	Christian Ethic
1. The principle of the dignity of human life	Exodus 20:13	Matthew 5:21, 22
2. The principle of the traditional monogamous family	Genesis 2:21–24	Ephesians 5:22–23
3. The principle of common decency	Genesis 3:7, 21	Matthew 5:27–28 Ephesians 5:3–5
4. The principle of the work ethic	Genesis 3:19 Exodus 20:9–10	II Thessalonians 3:10
5. The principle of the Abrahamic covenant	Genesis 12:1–3	Romans 11:1–2
6. The principle of God-centered education	Deuteronomy 6:4–9	Ephesians 6:4
7. The principle of divinely ordained establishments		
a. The home	Genesis 2:21–24	Ephesians 5:22–33
b. State or civil government	Genesis 10:32	Romans 13:1–7
c. Religious institution	Exodus 25:8–9 (tabernacle/temple)	Matthew 16:17–19 (church)

Then you oppose a Christian republic?

I believe that the American republic was built upon the principles of the Old and the New Testament. But I do not believe in a theocracy. I do not believe in a government ruled over exclusively by Christians and dominated by the Christian philosophy—to the exclusion of pluralism.

As a Christian who believes the Bible to be the Word of God, it is my conviction that, in eternity, there will be a theocracy. I believe that Jesus Christ, the Messiah, will one day rule upon the throne of David. And I believe that all true worshippers of the Messiah will spend an eternity in that very wonderful and desirable theocratic Kingdom.

But I do not believe that such a "Christian republic" will ever be established upon this Earth. To attempt to develop such a government is ridiculous.

We Christians and Jews who believe in the Bible can have a strong spiritual influence upon our country. We can, through our beliefs and life-styles, inspire a very healthy climate in our society. But it must always be voluntary; it must always be spontaneous. It cannot be legislated.

If the Moral Majority believes in a pluralistic society, why is there a need for an organization to press a moral viewpoint?

I think you could pose that question to every special interest group in existence today. The answer is very simple. Our democratic republic is so constituted that every American, as a productive citizen, should be informed and involved. Good government is not accidental. Edmund Burke said: "All that is necessary for evil to triumph is for good men to do nothing." I believe that vigilance is the price of liberty. If our nation is to remain free, pluralistic, and moral, all committed Americans must have a voice.

Moral Majority exists because there is a large body of Americans out there who feel that Moral Majority is the most effective organization on the American scene today to keep this nation on course as far as traditional values are concerned.

Would you like to see a true Jewish-Fundamentalist Christian dialogue under the framework of Moral Majority?

As a matter of fact, that has already begun. There have been many private meetings between the leaders of Moral Majority and leaders of the Jewish community.

This dialogue has been very healthy. That is one reason why the Moral Majority cannot be a religious organization. If we are to be effective in coalescing Americans from various religious points of view, it is important that we remain a strictly political organization.

A number of Jewish rabbis and leaders participate in the Moral Majority and we have been able, through discussion, to heal various divisions that have occurred between Jewish and Christian spokesmen. Quite often we are contacted by Jewish and Christian leaders to bring together religious leaders on opposite sides of the fence who are having personality differences. We are glad that we can serve in this way.

You have strong religious views, and you are also a politician. And your religion and your politics encroach upon each other. If you were to attain power—if the political Moral Majority were to gain power in this country—what assurances would a Jew, a Catholic, or a non-Evangelical Christian have that his interests would be secure?

First of all, let me once again state that no such situation will ever develop. The Moral Majority is not seeking to gain power in this country. We are attempting to have an influence upon the moral direction of the nation and we do want to see traditional moral values reinforced in this country. But Jerry Falwell is not interested in political office. I know of no one in Moral Majority who wants political power.

America was founded by persons who were seeking religious liberty. The colonists came here to escape the kind of tyranny that limited their ability to worship God as they pleased. The Puritans and Pilgrims who came here were the Evangelicals and Fundamentalists of their day. If there is any group on the face of the Earth that should be committed to religious liberty for all persons—namely, pluralism—it would be Evangelicals and Fundamentalists.

And could you personally vote for a non-Fundamentalist Christian?

President Reagan is a Presbyterian. I voted for him. Former President Carter declares himself an Evangelical Baptist. I did not vote for him.

I do not vote along party lines. I vote for the candidate who, in my opinion, is committed to the values that are dearest to my heart. There is no such thing as a perfect candidate just as there is no such thing as a perfect preacher of the Gospel. We are all human beings with our own weaknesses and frailties.

I could easily vote for a Roman Catholic President, a Jewish President, a Protestant President—whoever that man or woman might be who best represents the views and the values that are important to me as a voter.

There is an 80-year-old man who is a member of the Thomas Road Baptist Church which I pastor. He is a very godly man. He has had very little education. He previously worked on the railroad and retired as a bread truck driver. He has, for a number of years, served as a visitation pastor with our congregation. He visits homes and hospitals on a regular basis. Whenever I have a personal need or problem, I usually call Brother Worley first to ask for his prayers on my behalf. I have that kind of confidence in him.

I also know a very capable neurosurgeon. He is an atheist; or at least he says he is. If I am ever diagnosed as having a brain tumor, Brother Worley will not be asked to perform the surgery. I will ask my atheist neurosurgeon friend to perform the surgery . . . and I will ask Brother Worley to pray for him while he does it.

Do you have plans to continue the work you've done to seek the election of your own kind of candidates and to seek to remove candidates that you feel are diametrically opposed to your political position?

The Moral Majority does not endorse candidates. There are certain groups on the so-called Christian right who do endorse candidates. Some of them operate political action committees and finance candidates. There is nothing wrong with this practice. However, in the past Moral Majority has not pursued this approach.

I personally endorsed Ronald Reagan in the 1980 election. I have endorsed and supported many candidates for various offices—as a private individual. I do not endorse candidates on behalf of the Church which I pastor or on behalf of the Moral Majority. I do it as an individual. I also am quite involved personally in the political process in other ways. I think that every American citizen should be.

In the future, I will continue to be an active, involved, and informed participant in the political process. I will work for those candidates who represent the views and values that I appreciate. I will work against those candidates who do not hold to those views. This is exactly what labor unions, feminists, abortionists, and other special interest groups have done for years. It is healthy. It is desirable.

Is it an erroneous belief that both the Moral Majority and you personally were publicly on record as supporting Ronald Reagan?

It is not erroneous that I was on record as supporting Ronald Reagan. But Moral Majority was not on record supporting Ronald Reagan. In my opinion a vast majority of the membership of Moral Majority did, in fact, vote for Ronald Reagan. They also voted for many other pro-life, pro-family, and pro-Israel candidates.

Are you pleased with the moral performance of the Reagan Administration so far?

Moral Majority does not consider itself to be the moral watchdog of government. We did not call for the resignation of members of Congress involved in ABSCAM or in the recent morals scandals. We certainly take a stand on moral issues. But we leave the future of politicians to their own voting constituencies back home. It is not our role to condemn Senator Kennedy for Chappaquiddick or Richard Nixon for Watergate. It is our responsibility to give support and reenforcement to the moral and traditional values on which the nation was built.

We are very pleased with the fact that President Reagan has used the White House as a bully pulpit for most of the moral and social issues. He has spoken out often on issues of pornography, abortion, and the family. We could not be more pleased with the performance of the President in those areas.

The President has addressed these moral and social issues while feverishly attempting to rebuild the military defenses of this nation—which were in shambles when he took office—and to rejuvenate the national economy. He is proving successful on every front at this juncture.

Do you have a hit list of congressmen and senators whom you oppose?

No. We have never had a hit list. Several groups on the new right have hit lists. Christian Voice, I understand, published a list of senators and congressmen whom they wanted to see defeated in 1980. It is my feeling they were within their legal boundaries in doing so. This is nothing different from what labor unions, feminists, and others do on a regular basis.

However, Moral Majority has chosen not to do this. We were blamed for the political defeat of McGovern, Bayh, Church, and many other liberal members of Congress. It is true that many of our Moral Majority members voted against these liberal politicians because of their bad voting record on moral and social issues. But we do not have a hit list. We did not instruct our people whom to vote against.

Jesus said, "Render unto God the things that are God's and unto Caesar the things that are Caesar's." And Dr. Billy Graham is very concerned about the Moral Majority politicizing the Gospel. Why are you politicizing the Gospel?

I have not politicized the Gospel. What I do as pastor of the Thomas Road Baptist Church and speaker of the Old-Time Gospel Hour television and radio ministry is spiritual. What I do as a private citizen in the Moral Majority is political. As a Christian minister, I render my service unto God. As a private citizen, I render my service unto Caesar of government.

By the way, Billy Graham told me that he has never opposed the Moral Majority. I had a recent letter from Billy Graham in which he makes this clear. Here is what he said:

Dear Jerry:
I am deeply disturbed that there seems to be an attempt to drive a wedge between us. I'm deeply grateful for your faithful proclamation of the Gospel of Jesus Christ, the same Gospel I preach, and feel that all of us who know and love our Lord Jesus Christ need to stand together. Only Christ can bring hope to our troubled world. Our proclamation of Him must have first priority. I share your deep concern for the moral and spiritual issues which face the world today and for the alarming drift away from Biblical standards in public and private lives. I thank God for your boldness and pray that He will continue to give you wisdom and courage. Our nation needs to be warned that God has brought judg-

ment in the past to nations which have renounced moral law and He will do it again. If ever a nation needs spiritual revival, it is America.

In recent months, I have discussed both in private conversations and in media interviews in Japan, the United States, and more recently, Europe, the fact that the term "Moral Majority" has often been misunderstood and that some, for example, think that it is exclusively a white Protestant organization with racial overtones—one which has no concern for some of the deeper social issues which face our world. Over and over again, especially in other countries, I have explained that this is a faulty picture, and that it is composed of people from a cross-section of our pluralistic nation including Protestants, Catholics, Jews, and various ethnic groups who are concerned about the moral drift in our country.

Sincerely,
Billy

The national media has attempted to drive a wedge between Billy Graham and the Moral Majority. No such division exists.

Tell us about your ministry, your Church, your university.

I am pastor of the Thomas Road Baptist Church in Lynchburg, Virginia. I founded this Church in June of 1956 with 35 charter members. We presently have 20,000 members in a city of 63,000.

The Old-Time Gospel Hour television and radio ministry is our largest outreach. The Sunday morning worship service at the Thomas Road Baptist Church is videotaped and then aired on approximately 400 television stations for one hour each Sunday. The radio ministry is heard one-half hour daily on approximately 500 stations across America.

We have an educational institution composed of four schools. Lynchburg Christian Academy provides an accredited education for children attending kindergarten, elementary, and high school. Liberty Baptist College is an accredited liberal arts college. Liberty Baptist Seminary offers graduate work in various theological areas. The Institute for Biblical Studies trains those persons who are interested in a study of the Bible without the normal liberal arts offerings. More than 6,000 students are now in attendance. These students come from all 50 states and 25 foreign countries presently.

The Church is also involved in mission ministry in 65 nations. We do extensive work with refugees and displaced persons. Our Liberty Baptist College young people are involved in an extensive inner-city ministry in New York, Philadelphia, Detroit, Washington, D. C., and Los Angeles. Each summer, they live in the homes of minority Church members. During the day they do physical work to help upgrade the neighborhoods. In the evening they conduct spiritual ministries.

We own and operate the Elim Home for Alcoholics here in Lynchburg, Virginia. For 23 years we have taken in, without charge, hundreds of alcoholic men for therapeutic and spiritual ministry.

We own and operate the Florence Crittendon

Home for unwed mothers which provides an alternative to abortion.

We own and operate the Family Center, a clothing and food ministry to the poor in our area. Many families depend on the Family Center for groceries, clothing, and professional services.

We operate a very large children's camp on Treasure Island, located near downtown Lynchburg, attended last summer by 6,500 children, ages 6-12, the majority underprivileged. A $15.00 weekly charge is made for those who can pay; the rest are accepted free. Camp Liberty operates on a similar format, but serves high school and college youth.

Isn't there some inevitable overlap between the Moral Majority and your ministry?

No. Moral Majority has separate offices and officers. Moral Majority has no religious function. It is in no way connected to the Thomas Road Baptist Church, the mother organization of our ministry.

I serve as President of the Moral Majority and Pastor of the Thomas Road Baptist Church. My performance with Moral Majority is as a private citizen. Obviously, many persons have difficulty distinguishing my dual role. This is understandable. However, legally and technically, there is no connection between the Moral Majority and my Christian ministry.

There are many people who believe the electronic church is a personal profit center for the electronic preacher. Would you be willing to submit your own statement and tax returns to the press for public scrutiny?

Yes, we already do this. Our annual audited financial statement is made available to the national media each year. Our local Lynchburg newspaper usually does an extensive article based upon our annual report. Beyond that, a financial statement is mailed to any interested person who requests this information. We are audited by a large national firm and belong to the National Religious Broadcasters (NRB) organization. The NRB maintains its own system of demanding financial accountability from its members.

I receive no remuneration from the Moral Majority. I am not involved in any side enterprise or business endeavor. My sole income is from the Thomas Road Baptist Church. As the pastor of this local church, I receive a $49,500 annual salary. The church also provides the parsonage in which I live and other expenses necessary for my ministry. I also earn income from book royalties.

Where do you fit within what is called the Fundamentalist Christian spectrum? There are 40 million Fundamentalist Christian Americans: that's the popularly published estimate. How many of these would you consider followers of your viewpoint and how many support you financially?

I think that the overwhelming majority of Fundamentalist and Evangelical Christians in America share the moral positions of the Moral Majority, Inc. This is not to say that a majority of these Christians are members of the organization named Moral Majority.

Our religious and political enterprises have 7.5 million families on computer mailing lists. Assuming there are between three and four persons per household, 25 million individuals is a conservative estimate of the number of persons who are in actual contact with us by mail, telephone, and the media.

Recent Gallup polls indicate that 84 percent of all Americans still believe the Ten Commandments are relevant today. Additional polls indicate that America's youth are more conservative than their parents and are returning to the moral and traditional values of their grandparents. This would indicate that the 1980s is a decade of moral and spiritual rebirth for this country.

The bulk of your people are the poorly educated and disadvantaged economically. But
you also have as contributors the most wealthy oil people in this country. Where does the
bulk of your contributions come from and how
do the figures come out?

I would not agree that the bulk of our people are
poorly educated and disadvantaged economically. I
would acknowledge that millions of our people are
from the lower stratum of society as far as education
and finances are concerned, but would suggest that
the supporting audience for our ministries would be a
typical cross section of the population of this country.

We are grateful for large corporate support of our
endeavors. We are grateful for the grassroots support.
During the past fiscal year, approximately $100 mil-
lion was received by our collective ministries in cash,
properties and bequests. With the exception of several
major gifts, our average contribution was slightly
above $20.00. This would indicate a very broad base of
support.

What is your relationship to NCPAC, the organization that was established to oppose and
support certain select political candidates?

NCPAC, the National Conservative Political Action Committee, is an organization in Washington,
D.C., headed by Mr. Terry Dolan. This organization
endorses and opposes candidates, within the param-
eters of the law. It raises large sums of money for the

purpose of electing and preventing the election of certain candidates. And I find myself in general agreement with the candidates supported by NCPAC.

There is no connection between Moral Majority and NCPAC. I have met Mr. Dolan on several occasions. But we have had no legal or financial involvements at all with his organization. The Moral Majority is not a political action committee. We do not support or oppose candidates as such.

What is the relationship between the Moral Majority, yourself, and the Christian Round Table?

Mr. Ed McAteer, whom I know quite well, is the founder of the Christian Round Table. The Round Table is a conservative organization which defends and promotes the Judeo-Christian value system. I am one of 56 board members. I serve purely in an advisory role.

I have never had the privilege of attending a board meeting. I respect the efforts of Mr. McAteer and the Round Table and we have made several financial contributions to their efforts. Beyond that, there is no connection between the Moral Majority and the Christian Round Table.

What is your relationship with James Robison and what is his position on a Christian society?

James Robison is a Baptist evangelist who has

preached at the Thomas Road Baptist Church and to the students at the Liberty Baptist College. He is one of the spokesmen for the Christian Round Table. I cannot speak for Rev. Robison's views on a Christian society. I would guess them to be the same as mine.

Do you have any connection with any of the other evangelical ministers? People like Oral Roberts, Pat Robertson, or Jim Bakker?

I recognize these men, and many like them, as brothers in Christ. There is no legal or technical relationship between their ministries and ours.

I have met Pat Robertson on a number of occasions and have a very high regard for him. I particularly appreciate his open stand in support of the State of Israel. Oral Roberts and Jim Bakker take a similar stand in support of the State of Israel. I have met Oral Roberts and Jim Bakker only once or twice in my lifetime and assume that their stand on moral issues would be very similar to mine.

What part should the mass media play in establishing the proper moral tone of this country, and how well do you think they have carried out their task?

The mass media—television, radio, and print journalism—much like ministers in the church pulpits, have a great responsibility. We are all leaders of people and molders of public opinion. With this awesome responsibility, we must be very careful to exert a very positive and healthy effect on society. Unfortunately, in an attempt to be objective and pluralistic, the media has gone overboard to the left on most moral, social, and political issues in recent years.

Public Opinion magazine recently released the findings of a poll taken of a large number of journalists, commentators, and television anchor persons. They were asked their views on most of the moral and social issues. The overwhelming majority of these persons were positioned to the left of the American public.

During 1982, the entire national media distorted the Israeli liberation efforts in Lebanon and presented Israel as an invader rather than a liberator. This is a typical example of the leftist leanings of the media. Most Americans remember how Arafat and the PLO, the Syrians, and other enemies of Israel were looked upon as innocent bystanders victimized by the Israeli insurgents who came into Lebanon. The fact was just the opposite. But the entire American public was presented a warped picture which hurt the international image of Israel at that time.

When one looks at the position the media takes on abortion, pornography, and the traditional family, it is also easy to see that the national media is far to the left of the value system held by the American public. The mass media has an obligation to be more responsible in its presentation of traditional values. I have worked earnestly to help bring the television networks back into line with their responsibilities in this area. With the exceptions of "The Waltons" and "Little House on the Prairie," there have been very few prime-time programs which present traditional families in a happy and loving setting. We are not asking for a return of "Father Knows Best" and "Ozzie and Harriet." We are asking for fewer bedroom scenes, less gratuitous sex, and an elimination of unnecessary violence.

A leading liberal Christian theologian accused you and the Moral Majority of attempting to purchase a television network and make it a Christian network. Is there any truth to this and do you see anything wrong, in theory, with a religious organization owning a TV network?

I read a story by Ben Stein in the *Saturday Review* to the effect that Jerry Falwell and Moral Majority, with the support of a number of millionaires and billionaires such as Bunker Hunt, were contemplating purchasing controlling stock in ABC. This was the first I heard of the matter. There was no truth in the story whatsoever.

I have no interest at all in purchasing or controlling any television network. However, I see nothing wrong with religious Americans becoming involved in the media. I also see nothing wrong with persons committed to the free enterprise system becoming more involved in purchasing financial interests in networks.

In a recently published interview, you reported television as being an "act of the almighty dollar." What is the connection between television and money?

I don't recall exactly in what context I made that statement, but I think it is generally true. Much of prime-time television has deteriorated into something less than wholesome programming, and the almighty dollar is the major factor behind it. To take just one example, the soap operas in the afternoon are very seamy and injurious to traditional family values.

I understand that ratings are important and fully understand the role that the sponsors play in determining the kinds of programs that are aired. Most of the major sponsors of prime-time television are headed by persons who are committed to strong family values. All that is necessary to correct the problems of gratuitous sex and violence on television is for a voice to emerge demanding change. I remember with pleasure the statement made by Owen B. Butler, Board Chairman of Procter and Gamble, when he called for an improvement in this area by the television networks. Good things have begun to happen and during the past two years healthy moves have been made towards correcting the problem.

You seem to be talking about a boycott of television. Is that right? There have been other boycotts against the networks and they haven't been particularly effective. Why should the effort you are involved in be successful where others have failed?

Yes, we have been talking of a boycott. Nearly three years ago, the Coalition for Better Television, composed of hundreds of civic and citizens organizations, approached the networks to ask for a reversal of trends toward gratuitous sex and excessive violence on the screen. The networks ignored it. We then went to more than 100 of the major prime-time sponsors and found open doors and hearts. At that time, the major sponsors brought pressure on the networks. The networks began to clean up their act. Although much is yet to be done, it is encouraging that our own surveys indicate a move in the right direction by all three networks. We congratulate them. We are hopeful this trend will continue.

It sounds as if you want to dictate to television what goes on and what stays off.

We do not want to dictate to the networks what should be aired and what should not be aired. We simply want—as other special interest groups are doing—to influence the networks so that they do not offend the good taste of most American viewers. That is exactly what the PTA has done for years in the area of violence on television. That is exactly what feminist groups have been doing regarding the image of women. It is not censorship that we want; it is responsibility on the part of network leadership.

Regarding television programming, you refer generally to your concerns about foul language and scenes of questionable taste. Could you be a little more specific?

May I say to you that, first of all, I don't have time to watch much TV, except for sports—I make time for that. But that's not because I am against television. We have two or three in our house, but my family watches television selectively. We're not nuts about it or fanatics. We believe that nothing is innately good or bad. It depends on how it is used. You want *me* to be more specific about what *you* should like or dislike. I wouldn't want to do that. I don't think that I as—one person—can; but I think a consensus can. I certainly wouldn't name a program, an actor, or a network. I think that all of that has to be left to the millions of people who are watching television every night and coming to the conclusion that what they see is offending them. It is inevitable that a force like that will organize and make its opinion felt.

If the Coalition for Better Television discovers that the majority of the women watch and enjoy soap operas, would you soften your objection to them?

This is precisely what we are seeking. We want the people to have on television what they really want, not what some few writers and television directors think they should have.

Again, all the polls indicate that the American public is turned off by the efforts of Norman Lear and others to bring playboy-type programs to television. "Entertainment Tonight" recently revealed the findings of its own poll on such a subject. Overwhelmingly, the American public feels that the networks have gone too far.

What is your position on prayer in the schools? Doesn't allowing prayers in public schools undermine the separation of church and state?

I favor the return of voluntary prayers to the public schools. I oppose mandated or officially written prayers. Since 96 percent of all Americans believe in God, there should be a time in each day, when children may voluntarily participate in an unwritten prayer. And the people in that class who so wish should have the right to honor or absent themselves from that occurrence. President Reagan's proposed Constitutional amendment for voluntary prayer was quite well worded. It stated that no child should be denied the right of prayer or forced to pray. That is what I believe.

But what about the rights of the individual—that 4 percent, to take your figures, which does not pray. Can't you envision a situation in which a shy little ten-year-old kid, the only one in his class who chooses to remain silent, is put under such pressure by his classmates that his "free" choice disappears? Should we open kids up to potential intimidation?

I fully agree with President Reagan's statement in the Rose Garden last year when he said: "I have never known a child who was hurt by exposure to a voluntary prayer." During the 1940s, the principal of the elementary school I attended conducted a weekly chapel and invited a local minister to speak to us. I shall always be grateful for the impact this experience had on my life. My respect for God and sacred things was developed during those early years of elementary school. I was not damaged in any way.

What is your feeling about the trend within the society toward the glorification of sex?

During the 1960s and 1970s sex became a god in this nation. Women were exploited by the pornographers. Marriage became something to be held in disdain.

Sex is a very beautiful thing. God created and ordained that sex should be enjoyed within the marriage bond. There has never been a time in human history when sex was not an important part of God's program for the human race. However, love has been replaced by lust. Promiscuity on the part of heterosexuals and homosexuals has produced an epidemic of venereal diseases including Herpes and AIDS. Hollywood and the television industry must accept a great deal of the blame. The porn publishers must likewise stand guilty before God and this nation.

How do you feel about birth control, about the use of contraceptives?

I believe responsible birth control is a sensible means of family planning. Abortion is not birth control but rather the destruction of human life. Most of the popular birth control methods prevent the initiation of human life and, therefore, in my opinion, violate no moral codes.

Are all modern methods of contraception acceptable to you?

Those forms of contraception which destroy a fertilized egg are, in my opinion, similar to other types of abortion. It is my theological conviction that life begins with conception. Most of the modern methods of contraception, however, do not destroy conceived life.

Do you feel that sex education has a place in the schools?

I favor sex education in the public schools when taught as biological science. I believe that young people need basic information regarding reproduction, puberty, and anatomy. However, the social engineers have attempted to use sex education and what they often call "values clarification" to teach amoral and often *anti*moral values.

Many of these so-called sex education classes are nothing more than academic pornography. Homosexuality is often presented as an acceptable alternate lifestyle. Premarital and extramarital sex are often presented as acceptable ways of life. In other words, the typical sex education class in the public schools today is nothing more than a platform to teach moral positions that are foreign to those views held by most American parents. I object to this.

How do you feel about supplying contraceptives and birth control information to teenagers?

I am in favor of parents knowing what their children are doing. I favor rules which would require government-funded health agencies to inform parents before tampering with their children. I am totally opposed to tax dollars being used for the supply of contraceptives to teenagers. As far as birth control information is concerned, I am afraid that most of it is very slanted and is often damaging to the young people who receive it.

Planned Parenthood is one such government-funded organization involved in this field. Planned Parenthood operates abortion clinics. It presents abortion as the only reasonable alternative to an unwanted pregnancy. It further looks on free sex from a very amoral perspective.

You are on record as being against abortion. Can you envision any circumstances in which you might support abortion?

Abortion is a viable option when the life of the mother is at stake. This, as I see it, is a situation involving self-defense. The husband and wife have to make a moral decision regarding the survival of the mother or the survival of the child.

From a pragmatic perspective, I feel that rape and incest must be added to the life of the mother in any human life legislation if it is to become the law of the land. This does not mean I condone abortion in cases of rape and incest. Human life legislation allowing for abortions only in the case of rape, incest, and the life of the mother would essentially prevent more than 90 percent of all abortions now being performed. Since more than 1.5 million babies are being aborted annually in this country, more than 1.4 million human lives would be saved by this kind of legislation.

If abortion is murder, what criminal penalties would you see imposed on the American female who practices abortion and on her doctor?

I have never even considered such a situation. I believe that abortion is the taking of human life. I do not believe that any criminal action against a mother involved in an abortion is sensible or reasonable. I do believe that some criminal action should be taken against medical doctors who practice abortions—that is, if abortion were illegal.

You come across as condemning those who are on the opposite side of the human life amendment. Don't you see something distasteful in censuring someone for taking a moral position which happens to be at odds with yours? Isn't there something wrong with legislating morality?

In the Christian ministry, we do not condemn persons because of wrongdoing. Jesus Christ set the example by condemning sin but loving sinners. Christians should live the life of forgiveness toward all persons.

However, I feel that someone must stand up and speak out for the civil and human rights of the unborn. These millions of defenseless babies who have died since the Roe vs. Wade Supreme Court ruling of 1973 which legalized abortion on demand have had their human rights violated. It is not a matter of condemning persons who favor abortion. It is rather a matter of standing up for a voiceless minority of millions of unborn babies who are dying in this country throughout the years. I personally believe abortion is the national sin of America.

I often compare the silent biological holocaust going on in this country—called abortion— with the terrible holocaust that occurred in Hitler's Germany many years ago. That was a silent holocaust too. The rest of the world was kept unaware of the horrible things that were happening in Germany at that time. Six million Jews died. And 13 million little unborn babies have died in this country thus far. Something must be done.

You believe in the inerrancy of Scripture, and I assume that you have looked to Scripture in formulating your position on abortion. You label abortion as murder, on the assumption that the fetus is considered to be a life from the moment of conception. And yet, if one goes back to the Bible, in the reference to the fetus in Exodus 21:22, 23, it says that if two men quarrel and a pregnant woman nearby is hit in the process and she subsequently miscarries, the offender shall merely be fined. If, however, the woman is killed, then the guilty man too shall be killed. Thus, the Bible would seem not to consider a fetus prior to birth to be a full human life.

The King James Version on this passage states, "so

that her fruit depart from her." The Hebrew word for "depart" literally means "to bear, to beget, to bring forth." Thus, the phrase mentioned in Exodus 21:22, 23 may be translated "so that she gives birth prematurely." The New King James Version and the New International Version translate this verse this way. There is more grammatical evidence for premature birth than miscarriage in this text. At any rate, one is very hard-pressed to prove that this text in Exodus refers to miscarriage.

In order to get the true meaning of Scripture, it is necessary to take all the available evidence and not just an isolated verse of Scripture. There is much Biblical evidence to support the fact that life begins at conception and that unborn life is just as precious as born life. For example, in Psalms 139:13–16, David said in essence: I was formed in the conjugal act, the secret act. You knew me. You wrote my name down. And while I was yet unformed—that is while the fetus had no hands and no feet, while just the two elements of life existed—you knew me. You wrote my name down.

And then, through the period of gestation, David further says: "Oh how fearfully and wonderfully we are made." Since God writes our name down at the time of conception, I believe it is fair to assume that a real person exists at that time. In Jeremiah 1:5 the prophet says: "Before thou camest forth out of the womb I sanctified and ordained thee a prophet unto the nations." There are many other such passages.

In the New Testament, when Elizabeth and Mary came together for conversation, Elizabeth was already six months pregnant with John the Baptist. Elizabeth said to Mary, who was only several days pregnant with the Lord Jesus Christ, "the babe leaped in my womb as soon as the voice of thy salutation sounded in mine ears for joy" (Luke 1:44). So, from both the Old and the New Testament, Scripture supports the fact that the fetus is a live human being. I say that because I believe it from my heart.

There is adequate medical evidence, as well, that life begins at conception. Bernard Nathanson's book, *Aborting America*, is an excellent reference on this subject. To my knowledge, he himself, though a Jew, does not openly profess any belief in God. Yet, he tells of the days he operated a very busy abortion clinic. He gives his own personal testimony of how he became convinced that he was destroying human life. He is now an open advocate for the preciousness of unborn human life.

If equally religious hearts can hear God differently on specific issues, how can you say that there is only one way on abortion? I hear Exodus say this; you hear Psalms say that. We can differ and argue. The point is that since equally sincere people listening to God can have different views, why do you not allow the choice to remain?

I am well aware that many good people hold to the pro-abortion view. Others oppose abortion but favor the privilege of women making their own choice regarding abortion. I do not look on these persons as bad people. But, because of my commitment to relieving the plight of millions of unborn babies, I have asked

God to make my voice a clarion call for their civil rights.

In 1857, the Supreme Court by a 7-2 vote in the Dred Scott decision ruled that black people were not human beings. It further ruled that black persons could be bought and sold as chattel. The Supreme Court endorsed slavery. In 1973, that same court by the same margin, 7-2, ruled that unborn babies are not human beings. They have no human rights. They may therefore be destroyed like pieces of tissue. In my opinion, the Supreme Court was wrong both times.

When it was an issue, you were quoted as saying that God is against ERA.

I did not say that *God* was against the Equal Rights Amendment. I did say that *I* am against the Equal Rights Amendment. I personally support equal rights for all women. My wife is a pianist and an organist. Earlier in her life, she was a banker. My daughter, Jeannie, is now studying to become a medical doctor. I very much believe that women should earn the same wages for the same work as any man. I believe that women should have the same opportunity for advancement to any position or level of accomplishment.

The reason I have opposed the Equal Rights Amendment in the past is very simple. The ambiguous wording of the Equal Rights Amendment would have made it possible for the mandated drafting of women into combat—even against their will. I have always supported the right of women to volunteer for military service. Most women, however, are not made for

NFL football or combat. I do not believe that it is right to force those women into combat when they are not emotionally or physically equipped for it.

I further believe the Equal Rights Amendment would have penalized many American women financially. I think of those deserted wives who are left behind by a husband who has shunned his financial and parental responsibilities. The Equal Rights Amendment would have also sanctioned homosexual marriage. I opposed the Equal Rights Amendment and if it appears again in the same form as it did originally, I will oppose it again.

In view of the difficult times many minorities have had in obtaining their rights and just positions in society, are they entitled to any special consideration?

I think they are. I think that this government has, however, gone overboard in its attempts to correct some of its crimes against the Blacks, for example. Many black leaders oppose affirmative action. Many feel that special favoritism because of the color of one's skin is damaging to self-respect. I agree with that.

Some affirmative action has been good. But, as we attempt to help Hispanics, Blacks, women, the American Indian, and other minority groups in America, it is important that we do not violate the principle of self-worth and self-dignity. Most Americans want no more than the opportunity to learn, to achieve, and to succeed. We must guarantee that everyone has this opportunity.

You hardly started out as a liberal in your attitude toward Blacks. Could you tell us a little about your early racial views?

I was raised in a home that believed and practiced segregation. I was born in 1933 in Lynchburg, Virginia. I did not know anyone who was not a segregationist. But, as I have stated earlier, my personal experience with Jesus Christ as my Savior and Lord began a process of change in my attitude. As I grew spiritually in the years following my conversion, the Lord did for me what my environment had not done for me. At a point and time in my life I came to the place where I loved all persons in the same way God loves all persons.

It has been said that 15 years ago you opposed the civil rights movement and Martin Luther King's efforts. Can you comment on that?

I definitely opposed the involvement of ministers in marches, and other political activities in the early 60s. I held the mistaken view, at that time, that government and society would jointly correct all of the inequities that existed. Someone had told me as a young Christian that "religion and politics don't mix." I never bothered to ask for the book, chapter, and verse. I accepted this statement hook, line, and sinker. I remember preaching a sermon entitled "Ministers and Marches." I distributed that printed message. In that booklet, I urged my preacher friends to stay out of the streets and in their pulpits. That was in 1965.

Today, I find myself being criticized by liberal churchmen on much the same premise, I suppose, that I criticized Dr. King. I was wrong then. I changed my opinion. Things are not going to correct themselves. Ministers, as private citizens, must be more actively involved in moral change if in fact change is to occur.

What is your involvement with Blacks today?

Hundreds of Blacks attend the Thomas Road Baptist Church, which I pastor. The Liberty Baptist College and the schools also have several hundred minority students enrolled. I speak regularly in black churches across the nation. Recently, I produced a prime-time television program from the pulpit of the largest black congregation in Los Angeles. I think it is fair to say that our ministries have an absolutely open admissions policy.

What is your opinion about homosexuality?

It is my conviction that homosexuality is moral perversion. This is a Biblical view. Both Leviticus 18:22 and Romans chapter one support this position.

However, while I look on homosexuality as moral perversion, we reach out in love to help the homosexual. We have a staff of counsellors which includes one full-time psychiatrist and several psychologists. These persons are available for free counselling daily. Among those who come from across the nation for counselling are many homosexuals. Our counsellors first advise them that their lifestyle is wrong. They are then led to a personal relationship with God through the Lord Jesus Christ. They are given a great deal of spiritual and psychological help. Today, we can point you to many former homosexuals who are now living normal and healthy heterosexual life-styles. Some of these are now pastoring local churches.

If it were scientifically established to your satisfaction that there are many cases of homosexuality that are genetically induced and not socially or psychologically induced, would you change your attitude toward homosexuality?

In the first place, I do not believe that such a thing can be proven. One *chooses* to be promiscuous as a heterosexual or homosexual. One *chooses* his life-style. Most psychiatrists now agree that homosexuality is not inherited. Since one chooses his life-style as a result of environment, or sometimes as a result of situations beyond his control, it is also possible to opt out of that life-style. I personally feel that a genuine relationship with the Lord is essential to such a change.

Would you like to see your beliefs that God is against homosexuality translated into legislation?

Most of the states have laws which declare sodomy as illegal. However, like adultery, sodomy is a very difficult violation to deal with. I do not want to see government invading the bedrooms of the American people. But I do want to see America symbolically, at least, positioned against moral perversion. I want the United States to clearly take its legislative position on the side of the traditional family. I am not in favor of jailing or harassing persons because of their sexual orientation.

Along with the "right-to-life" question, there has arisen in recent years the "right-to-die" dilemma. What is your feeling about a person's right to die with dignity? Must we keep people for whom all joy has gone out of life alive just because we have the technological means to do so?

There is a great difference between using sufficient means to prolong one's life, and the actual practice of euthanasia or mercy killing.

I feel that, as professionals, we should do all we can to encourage living human beings to find meaning in life. It is true that depression and despondency are very real problems in the case of terminal illness. But I believe that we should be committed to helping people learn how to live rather than allowing them to opt for death. I would approach the "right-to-die" matter with great caution. We should be life-oriented.

Although it seems out of another century, there have been reports of late across the country of book burnings. And Moral Majority has been linked to some of them. Illinois Moral Majority Chairman, Rev. George Zarris, does not appear to be disturbed by the prospect of book burning. In his words: "Some stuff is so far out that you have to bend. I would think that moral-minded people might object to books that are philosophically alien to what they believe. If they have the books and feel like burning them, fine."

First of all, Moral Majority has never been involved in book burnings at any time. Secondly, George Zarris is a very intelligent young man and tells me that he has been misquoted in this case.

There have been book burnings in this country. Norman Lear found an alleged book burning in Virginia, Minnesota. He then produced a film and showed it nationwide attempting to deceive people into thinking that Moral Majority participated in that event. We found, with great effort, the pastor of a little Pentecostal church in Virginia, Minnesota, where this alleged book burning occurred. Actually, the young people of that church had conducted a youth revival. They became convinced that some of their musical LP albums were vulgar and detrimental to their spiritual development. Spontaneously, without pastoral encouragement, they decided to burn these LP albums in the church yard. A picture was made of this. Mr. Lear then inserted this into a movie entitled "Life and Liberty for Those Who Believe." He made every effort to link the Moral Majority and Jerry Falwell to this happening.

I am against book burning. It is significant, however, that most of the book burning and banning is being practiced by those from the left. Most of the convervative books which are committed to the Judeo-Christian tradition and to moral values have been removed from many public libraries nationwide. Feminists, for example, are writing their own Bible and removing all alleged "sexist" statements from their new Bible. Obviously, this is censorship and banning at the lowest level.

What about public libraries? Would you, therefore, condemn any attempts to remove books from libraries?

We do indeed object to the removing of books from libraries. As a matter of fact, we have been actively involved in attempting to put additional books on library shelves. Recently Moral Majority conducted a national campaign to request librarians nationwide to assure that all views were clearly represented on their library shelves. Our survey indicated that most conservative books were very poorly represented on the shelves.

I want to read a statement which you made concerning unemployment and poor people: "We feed them and encourage their laziness and their worthlessness and you can't give them a job because they can make more money on unemployment. The Bible says that a man who will not work, neither shall he eat. One of the members of this church, a wealthy man, gave me two Irish setters. He told me what kind of fresh meat they needed and where I could buy it. When he left, I went to the store and got me a 50-pound bag of Purina dry dog food. I put it out for them and sure enough they wouldn't eat it. Four days later they did. When we get these bums hungry enough, they will work."

First of all, that statement was not in reference to the poor. Taken in its proper context, I was referring to a number of persons who refused to work and who were being encouraged in their slothfulness by the continued welfarism directed their way. I very much support Social Security for the aged and indigent. I support welfare help for the truly needy. The Thomas Road Baptist Church owns and operates the Family Center. Presently, this Family Center is providing food and clothing for 700 poor families in the Lynchburg, Virginia, area. I do all I can to urge all pastors and churches to follow suit. However, there are many persons in America who are turned off to work because of an overdose of welfarism. I believe that "workfare" along with welfare is the proper approach.

At the close of our conversation, I asked Jerry Falwell what he saw as the ideal relationship between church and state.

The framers of the First Amendment said that Congress shall make no law regarding the establishment of a state religion. The founding fathers never wanted another Church of England dominating our society. Likewise, they said that Congress shall not forbid the free exercise of religion or tell people how, when, or where to worship. Therefore, the Constitution does not address the separation of church and state at all.

I believe that the practice of the principle of the separation of church and state is good. Generally, we have practiced that separation for about 200 years in this country. The practice should continue.

The Church is nothing more than people. There are millions of Americans who belong to churches and synagogues. I do not believe that church organizations should become politically involved. The World Council of Churches, the National Council of Churches, the United Church of Christ, and other liberal church organizations have been very much involved on the political scene for years. I discourage this. I would much rather challenge individual church members, as private citizens, to become involved.

Jesus Christ said: "Render to Caesar the things that are Caesar's and to God the things that are God's" (Mark 12:17). This is the challenge from our Lord to serve God through our religious institutions and to serve government through the political process. I believe one can perform both services with dignity and with honor.

Index